WOKE BRAND

From Selling Products to Fixing Society's Deep Issues

DR ABAS MIRZAEI

ARCHWAY
PUBLISHING

Archway Publishing books may be ordered through booksellers or by contacting:

Archway Publishing
1663 Liberty Drive
Bloomington, IN 47403
www.archwaypublishing.com
844-669-3957

Because of the dynamic nature of the Internet, any web addresses or links contained in this book may have changed since publication and may no longer be valid. The views expressed in this work are solely those of the author and do not necessarily reflect the views of the publisher, and the publisher hereby disclaims any responsibility for them.

Any people depicted in stock imagery provided by Getty Images are models, and such images are being used for illustrative purposes only. Certain stock imagery © Getty Images.

ISBN: 978-1-6657-3588-9 (sc)
ISBN: 978-1-6657-3589-6 (e)

Library of Congress Control Number: 2022923884

Print information available on the last page.

Archway Publishing rev. date: 02/15/2023

To my daughter Liliana, and my best friend, wife, and partner in life, Helen, who has always been my great support.

CONTENTS

1

Why This Book? Introduction

Until relatively recently, people wanted to buy high-quality cameras; low-maintenance, reliable, safe cars; and comfortable, soft, and durable shoes and activewear. In 2023 we want to buy cameras (to capture scenes of social injustice); shoes (that aren't made using child labor); and cars (that emit minimal carbon and are safe for the environment). Likewise, we purchase "animal-friendly" vegan handbags (that are not associated with animal cruelty) and use ride-sharing services (that promise not to exploit their drivers). Even if it means accepting a suboptimal or pricey product or service (in the short term), we are increasingly happy to make personal sacrifices to help create a better world.

That's why the commercial world is moving toward broadcasting its humane values and higher purpose and competing on virtue rather than price or quality. We all have seen examples of brands becoming "social justice warriors" and attempting to solve some of humanity's most intractable and deepest social and political issues overnight.

You might have started wondering if the commercial world is moving too fast. You've almost certainly begun wondering what the right thing to do is and what the role of a commercial brand is regarding addressing sociopolitical, environmental, and legal issues. Should a brand get engaged in those issues at all? If so, when and why? How far should they go? And whose interests should take precedence—members of historically oppressed groups, loyal customers, or employees or shareholders? What is the right balance (if it is even possible to balance these interests effectively)?

Then there are the most important questions of all, at least for brand and marketing managers: What is the risk of damaging the brand by trying too hard to change the status quo? Won't the brand be considered desperate and opportunistic?

That often leads to other perplexing questions: What was so wrong with corporate social responsibility (CSR)? Why do growing numbers of businesses and brands now feel the need to become "woke"?, which can be defined as being *alert to injustice in society, especially racism* (The Oxford Dictionary, 2017).

You wonder about those questions—and then you hear that a brand like Ben & Jerry's has announced it will stop selling ice cream in the Occupied Palestinian Territory (OPT). You may be incredulous at the thought of an ice cream brand sanctioning its customers and parachuting into a hugely divisive political and religious conflict. Surely that's risky?

If you're a brand manager, you realize you've been thinking about a range of possibilities for your next marketing and branding move and that none were about, for instance, improving the quality of offerings, launching an innovative new product or service, or removing a pain point in customer experience.

You sense that maybe you should leapfrog all this and find a nonfunctional focus for your next campaign. You intuit that functional offerings are dated, and no one will fall in love with your brand if you try to just sell functionality.

You start looking around, searching for the best recent examples. You soon notice most campaigns are now aspirational and motivational. Many are also controversial! It becomes apparent that people aren't just buying products or services anymore. Instead, they're buying inspiring quotes and emotionally arousing messages.

You continue thinking about creative ideas for your next branding move. You go back to not promoting product features but rather championing humane values. You realize consumers are no longer interested in a shampoo that makes their hair shinier; they want one that is inclusive and will help end racism or prevent global warming.

Congratulations! Your thoughts are officially starting to become woke.

Woke branding has become the new wave that brand and marketing managers can no longer avoid. In getting woke, fighting discrimination, and questioning the status quo, there are questions to ask, steps to follow, and considerations to take note of.

Avoid going woke, and your brand risks irrelevancy, especially with younger consumers.

Yet if you go woke, you're likely to experience a backlash.

Woke Activist Brand (which I define here as the brand being awake and alert to discrimination and injustice) unpacks the dynamics of woke branding, identifies the ingredients of wokeness, and offers a roadmap for those wanting to walk into the uncertain world of wokeness with minimal risk.

This book is the outcome of three years of active listening and monitoring of the public conversation. I've analyzed hundreds of thousands of comments left on social media and many online debates about woke (or woke-ish) branding moves.

This book is neither a pro-woke nor an anti-woke polemic. Instead, with the appropriate critical distance, it presents a range of different views about wokeness.

There are several characters, ranging from the woke to the indifferent to the decidedly non-woke. You may find yourself resonating more closely with one of the following four characters more than others.

- Nonbeliever opposer
- Diehard supporter
- Interpreter
- Careless

Wherever you fall on this woke-to-anti-woke spectrum, I hope this book will provide you with practical insights into topics such as the differences between CSR, purpose, woke, woke authenticity, woke sacrifice, and many other concepts.

If you're weighing the risks of engaging in woke moves and aren't sure about the dynamics of consumer response and the steps to take, then this book is for you.

2

Where Woke Came from and Where Woke Is Headed

Where Woke Came From

First used in the 1940s, the term *woke* has resurfaced in recent years as a concept that symbolizes awareness of social issues and movement against injustice, inequality, and prejudice. Being woke was originally associated with African Americans fighting racism but has been appropriated by other activist groups—taking it from awareness and blackness to a colorless and timeless phenomenon.

Woke History

In their ongoing fight against racism and social injustice, Black Americans have used the term *woke* at key moments in history. In literal terms, being woke refers to being awake and not asleep. Urban Dictionary defines woke as "being aware of the truth behind things 'the man' doesn't want you to know."

Meanwhile, a concurrent definition at Lexico signals a shift in meaning to "the act of being very pretentious about how much you care about a social issue."

The Oxford Dictionary expanded its definition in 2017 to add it as an adjective meaning "alert to injustice in society, especially racism."

In the first volume of *Negro Digest*, published in 1942, J. Saunders Redding used the term in an article about labor unions.[1] Twenty years later, a 1962 *New York Times* article about the woke movement was published: If You're Woke You Dig It.[2]

On June 14, 1965, Martin Luther King Jr. gave a commencement address called Remaining Awake through a Great Revolution[3] at Oberlin College, where he said, "Remaining awake is among the greatest challenges of those graduating today."

Fast-forward to 2008, when Erykah Badu sang "I stay woke" in her popular song "Master Teacher." In July 2012, Badu tweeted a message to "stay woke" in solidarity with Russian rock group Pussy Riot,[4] extending the fight for social injustice to another context.

6

From February 26, 2012, to April 19, 2015, a sequence of incidents brought attention to the treatment of young Black Americans by police and sparked an eruption in social justice and equality activism. In summer 2013, after George Zimmerman was found not guilty of killing teenager Trayvon Martin,[5] the hashtag #BlackLivesMatter was created, urging people to stay woke and be conscious of race struggles.[6]

A review of Google keywords shows the search for defining wokeness surged after 2015, with phrases such as "defining woke," "woke meme," "woke urban," and "woke define" used. By September 2016, the phrase Black Lives Matter had been tweeted more than thirty million times, according to Twitter[7].

The phrase "stay woke" gained strength and became a symbol of movement and activism. Staying woke became the umbrella purpose for movements like #BlackLivesMatter (fighting racism), #MeToo (fighting sexism and sexual misconduct), and #NoBanNoWall (fighting for immigrants and refugees).

Where Woke Is Headed

Even though the concept of woke came from African Americans' fight against social injustice, the spillover of the word *woke* to other types and forms of social injustice and discrimination has been profound. Any inclusion and diversity program and initiative are now labeled as a woke move, regardless of its associations with African Americans. In fact, any progressive move, no matter what the context and concept, is now labeled as woke. From Minnie Mouse's outfit,[8] to M&M's rebrand celebrating inclusion, to Neo Green Socialists in Downing Street, woke has moved to contexts with no association to African Americans.

Part of this migration of the word woke to other contexts has been fueled by those opposing wokeness. Mostly mocking and ridiculing the concept, opposers have labeled any progressive move as woke, contributing to the expansion of the usage of the word in different situations.

Going forward, wokeness will become a popular cultural product and the umbrella reference to all purposeful progressive moves.

References

1   Google Books. 2022. *Black World/Negro Digest*. https://books. google.com/books?id=MbIDAAAAMBAJ&printsec=frontcover &source=gbs_ge_summary_r&cad=0#v=onepage&q&f=false.

2   William Melvin Kelley. If You're Woke You Dig It; No Mickey Mouse Can Be Expected to Follow Today's Negro Idiom without a Hip Assist. *New York Times,* May 20, 1962. https://timesmachine.nytimes.com/ timesmachine/1962/05/20/140720532.html?pageNumber=332.

3   Andrew Belonsky. MLK Jr. on Getting "Woke" in 1965. https:// incaseyoureinterested.com/2019/01/21/mlk-jr-on-getting-woke-audio/.

4   Charles Pulliam-Moore. How "Woke" Went from Black Activist Watchword to Teen Internet Slang. *Splinter News.* January 8, 2016. https://Splinternews.com/How-Woke-Went-From-Black-Activist-Watchword-To-Teen-Int-1793853989.

5   K. G. Bates. A Look back At Trayvon Martin's Death, and the Movement It Inspired. *NPR.* July 31, 2018. https://www.npr.org/ Sections/Codeswitch/2018/07/31/631897758/A-look-back-at-Trayvo n-Martins-death-and-the-movement-it-inspired.

6   Mirzaei, Abas. "Where 'woke came from and why marketers should think twice before jumping on the social activism bandwagon." *The Conversation,* August 2019.

7   Jenna Wortham. Black Tweets Matter: How the Tumultuous, Hilarious, Wide-Ranging Chat Party on Twitter Changed the Face of Activism in America. *Smithsonian Magazine.* September 2016. https://www. smithsonianmag.com/arts-culture/black-tweets-matter-180960117/.

8   Monika Barton. Disney Fans Furious over Minnie Mouse's "Woke" Outfit Change into "Sustainable Pantsuit." *NewsHub*, January 28, 2022. https://www.newshub.co.nz/home/entertainment/2022/01/ disney-fans-furious-over-minnie-mouse-s-woke-outfit-change-i nto-sustainable-pantsuit.html.

3

Is Woke Brand Activism Good for Society?

Many people are cynical about woke corporate activism and have serious reservations for brands' deep-down motivations in engaging with sociopolitical issues. While this book is not simplistically pro-woke, it does argue that it can benefit a society to have powerful corporations champion social justice and antidiscrimination causes. More on that shortly. But first, let's explore the woke and anti-woke schools of thought.

Author Viewpoint

Different Schools of Thought

School 1

Those in School 1 believe brands should stick to their knitting and focus on improving their offerings. In practice, this means making their ice cream tastier, designing more comfortable shoes, and explaining why their razors are justifiably expensive. If this is you, you probably don't want to be lectured by for-profit businesses. You are bemused that multinationals living in glass houses think they can throw virtue-signaling stones to try to move more units.

If you are a white, heterosexual, conservative male, you may feel you are under siege in a culture that you perceive as celebrating non-whiteness, LGBTIQA+ individuals, and women. You may fear for your own future, economic and otherwise, in an age when most big businesses and public sector organizations have enthusiastically signed up to the diversity, equity, and inclusion agenda.

Those in School 1 may have looked on in amusement as Starbucks' "Race Together" campaign went wrong and when Pepsi showcased their sugary drink in a tone-deaf ad that borrowed imagery from Black Lives Matter (BLM) protests. You probably weren't won over by Airbnb's "We Accept" campaign, which combined many races and skin tones in one headshot.

But it would be wrong to assume School 1 only contains

angry white males. Indeed, many non-Caucasian males, LGBTIQA+ individuals, and women can find woke branding. These individuals may not want to be reduced to their skin color, sexuality, or gender and may not welcome brands' often ham-fisted attempts at marketing to members of their community. For such individuals, being the target of woke advertising—such as McDonald's flipping its M into a W to celebrate International Women's Day—feels uncomfortably like being a diversity hire.

School 2

If you're in School 2, you're super excited to see brands are finally featuring your race or gender, look, and skin tone in their campaigns. You're excited Cinderella isn't white and blonde anymore and that you don't need to explain to your kids why there are no Black or brown Barbie dolls.

You used to feel helpless and hopeless seeing all the conventionally attractive people in ads, and you're delighted brands are now featuring people with a wider range of body shapes.

You're excited that Victoria's Secret has embraced diversity and now has "angels" who are dark-skinned, Asian, transgender, lesbian, and plus-sized. Now that Victoria's Secret has evolved, your child's dream of walking on the catwalk may still come true even if they aren't a tall, thin biological woman with white skin and blonde hair.

You're thrilled to see brands using their influence to become agents of change and to promote humane values. You're not naïve and you recognize that businesses need to make a profit to survive. Nonetheless, you're supportive rather than cynical about businesses seeking to make a profit in a new way. (Even if their profit-seeking motivations have not changed, their approaches in seeking profit certainly have.) You even dare to hope that the Bad Old Days of marketing campaigns objectifying women, misrepresenting certain ethnic groups, and encouraging overconsumption are drawing to a close. As far as you're concerned, even if brands are faking it, it's better than them not doing anything to improve society. If brands must "fake it until they make it," so be it. And of course, you don't understand why many of those in School 1 get so worked up about woke brands and woke corporations.

Both Schools of Thought Have Something to Offer

This book is built on reviewing the arguments advanced by both schools of thought. It provides responses to both schools' questions and criticisms. This book explains why, despite the valid reservations many have about commercial brands going woke, holding corporations more accountable in their involvement in social issues is, overall, a good thing. This book aims to convince the cynics that, on balance, woke capitalism is going to be beneficial for societies.

If you're currently in School 1, this book will attempt to convince you that the poor execution of woke marketing campaigns by a handful of opportunistic brands shouldn't stop you from supporting the corporate fight against social injustice.

In fact, this book throws at you the following two scenarios from which to choose.

Scenario 1

Here we have Nespresso's "What else?" campaign featuring George Clooney. Nespresso continues making a profit without being worried about the plight of coffee farmers and the effect of coffee farming on the environment.[1]

Scenario 2

Nespresso switches from its What else? campaign to "The choices we make," and "when coffee has the power to transform communities." This shows it is providing support to farmers but still results in Nespresso increasing its revenue.[2]

Which of the above scenarios do you think has the potential to be a target for cancel-culture activists? Which do you think has a greater likelihood of being criticized by consumers?

The core point of this book is that if brands don't expose themselves to the brand public through engaging in sociopolitical and environmental issues, if they don't put themselves in the spotlight, and if they remain silent, there is a lesser chance of them being called out by the public for their wrongdoing.

This book argues that being critical of brands' woke moves and discouraging them from involvement in political issues is actually good news for brands. They will use it as an excuse to go back to old-school persuasive, emotional-overload campaigns that try to sell consumers products they don't need, at prices they can't afford, so they can impress people they don't much care about.

If you're currently in School 2, this book argues that you shouldn't get too excited about superficial surface-level cute woke moves, especially when they don't involve substantial investment or potential financial sacrifices. The danger of superficial cute woke moves is that brands may get used to communicating surface-level woke activism and forget they must also practice what they preach. This book argues brands must go beyond *costless* virtue-signaling and show *costly* signaling moves—ones that risk profit and revenue—if they are truly concerned about addressing the challenges societies face. For brand and marketing practitioners, this book provides a roadmap to winning over School 1 consumers and holding on to and further impressing School 2 consumers.

This book's message to brand and marketing practitioners is that you won't succeed if you ignore or actively antagonize School 1 consumers to win over School 2 consumers. In fact, even School 2 consumers may turn against you if you are perceived to be opportunistically jumping on a bandwagon. Not winning

Author's Thesis & Goal

over School 1 consumers is a strategic mistake. Losing School 2 consumers is an even greater error.

This book warns against woke brands attacking one group to demonstrate its support of another group. It questions the "inclusive" marketing campaigns that try to replace white people with Black people, men with women, and heterosexuals with LGBTIQA+ individuals. Being woke, inclusive, and diverse isn't about getting rid of certain types of people; it's about adding in more types of people.

References

1   Gillian West (2013) Nespresso unveils latest campaign and new digital platform with George Clooney and Matt Damon, *The Drum*, November 7, 2013.
    https://www.thedrum.com/news/2013/11/07/nespresso-unveils-lates t-campaign-and-new-digital-platform-george-clooney-and-matt
2   When Coffee Has the Power to Transform Communities 6" | USA.
    https://www.youtube.com/watch?v=_3KGMVhkL4M&ab_channel=Nespresso

4

Consumer Brand Relationships

People tend to treat brands as if they're human and humanize them by attributing human characteristics to them.[1] Consumers tend to connect with brands that have humanlike features, personalities, and mindsets. Relying on visual or verbal cues, humans evaluate different brands as potential candidates with which to start a relationship, based on the extent to which their humanlike characteristics appeal.

We develop relationships with brands and bring our feelings to this relationship. The more humanlike the brand, the more we express our feelings of love (or, sometimes, hate). We give brands credit or blame them for their actions; we label them the "coolest" or "dumbest"; and we even troll them. They become the topic of our dinner table discussions.

Three Steps in Building Consumer Brand Relationships

The relationships between consumers and brands evolves in three stages.

Stage 1: Looking for humanlike characteristics.
Stage 2: Assessing the overlap between the self and brand's humanlike characteristics.
Stage 3: Falling for the brand and showing signs of brand attachment (as opposed to brand aversion).

MacInnis and Folks[2] offer a detailed review of how brands are humanized. Consumers first perceive humanlike features in brands. They may, for instance, see a humanlike name, gender, face, or voice (e.g., Amazon Alexa, the Michelin Man).

Hur, Koo, and Hofmann, examining the effect of anthropomorphized products (products with human features) on the extent to which dietary consumers wanted to eat a product, found that high-calorie cookies with human shapes and names reduced the conflict between consumption desire and self-control.[3]

In another study, it was found that in a word-completion

Human-like Brands

computer game, anthropomorphized laptop helpers (i.e., a laptop with a human face on its screen) reduced the level of players' enjoyment, since it reduced the perceived level of players' autonomy.[4] Besides tangible and objective humanlike brand features, in Stage 1 consumers look for subjective and conceptual humanlike cues, categorizing brands based on their personality traits. Previous research has proposed several brand personality categorizations to describe brands.

In evaluating brand personalities, consumers have different perspectives and motivations, so they form different conscious and subconscious expectations. Sociality and effectance motivations are the two key motivations for anthropomorphizing brands. People anthropomorphize objects because they have the desire for a social connection (sociality motivations), or they want to feel they have control and authority over their surroundings (effectance motivations).[5, 2]

As explained by implicit self-theory, consumers adopt one of the two types of theories in their relationships with brands: the *entity theory* or the *incremental theory*.

While *incremental theorist consumers* believe their personality is malleable and can be improved through their own efforts, *entity theorist consumers* believe their personality is fixed and they should rely on other objects, such as brands, to improve their personality, and to cover the gap between their actual personality and desired personality.[6]

Incremental theorist consumers see brands as a tool for self-improvement. With entity theorist consumers, brands become the hero in self-enhancement,[7] enabling the self to communicate its desired personality using brands with the same personalities (for instance, using a brand with a sophisticated personality to signal the self's desired personality of sophistication).

In a series of experiments, Park and John[7] found that entity theorist consumers who were using a Victoria's Secret shopping bag felt better looking and more glamorous. Likewise, those using an MIT pen felt more like a leader and more intelligent.

Brands & Personality

To take another example, brands with an underdog personality were found to be more appealing to consumers who felt like an underdog themselves.[8] Similarly, if consumers value dynamism and being active, embedding and signaling an active personality can facilitate the process of brand personification, which can result in a perception of a brand that is engaging, alert, lively, and full of energy.[9]

For both types of theorists, and in particular the entity theorist consumers—who seek self-enhancement and expansion in forms of personal and social expressions—the level of overlap between self-brand personalities becomes extremely important.

Things won't start getting serious between the self and the brand unless there is a high degree of congruity between brand personality and the self-personality. Once consumers perceive humanlike features in brands, in Stage 2 of the consumer-brand relationship, consumers start evaluating the extent to which those humanlike features and personalities are in sync with the self's personalities.

Previous research has identified four types of self-congruity: the congruity between brand personality and

a. the actual self;
b. the desired self;
c. the social self; and
d. the desired social self.[10]

Each of the four are driven by certain motivations that can be classified into two main categories of motivations: self-motive socialness and degree of self-enhancement sought.[10] Offering humanlike personalities with a high overlap with the self-personality can therefore contribute to self-brand relationship in four different levels, fulfilling the underlying needs of self-socialness, self-enhancement, and self and social consistency (the need to maintain oneself or social concepts). The congruity between the brand personality traits and the self's personality is crucial in further developing the relationship.

In Stage 3, when consumers discover that there is a great self-brand personality congruity and connection, they start expecting humanlike capacities from the brand, such as feelings and behaviors.[11, 12] Consumers in the final stage of the self-brand relationship adopt relational norms in their relationship with brands, similar to the norms that guide their relationships with other people (for example, exchange norms).[2]

The consumer-brand relationship can be developed in different levels of functional relationship (with utilitarian benefits in mind). There is the personal level: "I don't know why but I love/hate this brand"; and the social level: "I relate with the brand because it helps me to be seen the way I want to be seen" (e.g., rugged or compassionate).[13]

Research finds that even utilitarian benefits can be influenced by personal and social levels of customer-brand relationship. The more personal and social the relationship, the more meaningful the brand becomes to consumers. So a brand developing a relationship with its target audience on personal and social levels seems inevitable.

However, before moving to a social level of relationship, customers first develop a personal relationship. Therefore, personal relationship is the central level of the customer-brand relationship. Consumers try to develop a personal relationship through personifying brands and identifying the brand meaning with personality attributes.[14]

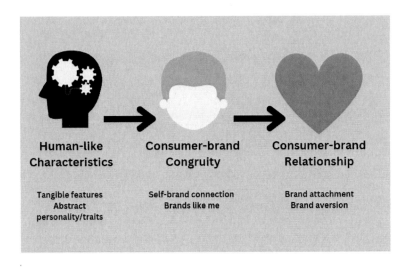

Human-like Characteristics

Tangible features
Abstract personality/traits

Consumer-brand Congruity

Self-brand connection
Brands like me

Consumer-brand Relationship

Brand attachment
Brand aversion

People are motivated to include other entities with similar characteristics and personalities in their selves, for self-expansion and enhancement purposes, and to achieve their goals. The greater the self-brand personality overlap, the closer, stronger, and more positive the relationship.[15, 16]

Thus, the more a brand is perceived as a tool for self-enhancement and self-expansion, the greater the self-brand attachment.

Similarly, but in the opposite direction, consumers who see a brand as a threat to self-contraction will avoid the brand and feel distant from it.[17] Like their relationships with humans, consumers' relationships with brands can vary from strong and positive (love) to strong and negative (hate). Park et al. propose the brand attachment-aversion relationship model between the self and the brand. Over time, consumers with different levels of feelings for or against a brand transit from one end of spectrum (attachment) to the other (aversion), while those consumers with no strong feelings toward a brand may feel neither attached nor distant and continue a neutral relationship in the brand indifference zone.[17]

Consumer-Brand Relationships

Aversion   Indifference   Attachment

Brand personality is a key reference point for the level of brand attachment versus brand avoidance in the self-brand relationship. Brands can adopt personalities from a variety of personality categories. Since the 1997 publication of Jennifer Aaker's seminal paper on brand personality conceptualization,[18] which offered categories such as sincerity, excitement, and ruggedness, others have tried to overcome the shortcomings of Aaker's brand personality dimensions, examining personality traits such as integrity and trendiness. Criticizing the lack of generalizability and its loose definition, [19, 20, 21] several researchers have provided alternative brand personality dimensions. Geuens et al. focus on attributes derived from human personality, proposing responsibility, activity, aggressiveness, simplicity and emotionally as dimensions of brand personality,[19] and propose three dimensions for brand personality, including favorability, originality, and clarity.[22]

Overall, according to Malone and Fiske, consumers' perception of brand personalities can be classified into two key categories: warmth (associated with brand characteristics) and competence (related to the brand's ability).[24] Most of the research on brand personality conceptualization and measurement has focused on the positive side of the brand attachment-aversion relationship model. However, negative personalities are equally, if not more influential in consumers' perceptions of brands.

While it is important to have clear and specific personalities that consumers can relate to, brands are realizing it is not enough to just be cool or sophisticated or adventurous. Not only do brands need to have humanlike characteristics, they should also act and behave like humans; they should assume humanlike responsibilities.

Becoming a woke activist has become a new avenue to build, maintain, and reinforce consumer-brand relationships. Brands are acting on social issues just like humans do. They are taking humanlike characteristics and emotion-based relationships to a whole new behavior-based level.

References

1   Aaker, David, *Aaker on Branding: 20 Principles That Drive Success* (New York: Morgan James Publishing, 2014).
2   MacInnis, Deborah J, and Folkes, Valerie S. 2017. "Humanizing Brands: When Brands Seem to Be like Me, Part of Me, and in a Relationship with Me," *Journal of Consumer Psychology*, *27*(3),355–74. DOI: 10.1016/j.jcps.2016.12.003
3   Hur, Julia D., Koo, Minjung. and Hofmann, Wilhelm. 2015. "When temptations come alive: How anthropomorphism undermines self-control". *Journal of Consumer Research*, *42*(2): 340-358.
4   Kim, Sara., Chen, Rocky P., and Zhang, Ke. 2016. "Anthropomorphized helpers undermine autonomy and enjoyment in computer games". *Journal of Consumer Research*, 43(2): 282–302.
    DOI: https://doi.org/10.1093/jcr/ucw016
5   Epley, Nicholas., Waytz, Adam. and Cacioppo, John T., 2007. "On seeing human: a three-factor theory of anthropomorphism". *Psychological review*, *114*(4), 864-886.
    DOI: 10.1037/0033-295X.114.4.864

6   Mathur, Pragya., Jain, Shailendra P., and Maheswaran, Durairaj. 2012. "Consumers' implicit theories about personality influence their brand personality judgments". *Journal of Consumer Psychology*, 22(4): 545–557.
     DOI: doi.org/10.1016/j.jcps.2012.01.005

7   Park, Ji K., and John, Deborah R. 2012. "Capitalizing on brand personalities in advertising: The influence of implicit self-theories on ad appeal effectiveness". *Journal of Consumer Psychology*, 22(3): 424–432.
     DOI: https://doi.org/10.1016/j.jcps.2011.05.004

8   Paharia, Neeru., Keinan, Anat., Avery, Jill., and Schor, Juliet. B. 2011. "The underdog effect: The marketing of disadvantage and determination through brand biography". *Journal of Consumer Research*, 37(5): 775–790.
     DOI: https://doi.org/10.1086/656219

9   Gordon, Ross., Zainuddin, Nadia. and Magee, Christopher. 2016. "Unlocking the potential of branding in social marketing services: Utilizing brand personality and brand personality appeal". *Journal of Services Marketing*, 30(1): 48–62.

10   Aguirre-Rodriguez, Alexandra., Bosnjak, Michael. and Sirgy, Joseph M. 2012. "Moderators of the self-congruity effect on consumer decision-making: A meta-analysis". *Journal of Business Research*, 65(8), 1179–88.
     DOI: https://doi.org/10.1016/j.jbusres.2011.07.031

11   Waytz, Adam., Cacioppo, John. and Epley, Nicholas., 2010. "Who sees human? The stability and importance of individual differences in anthropomorphism". *Perspectives on Psychological Science*, 5(3), 219–232.
     DOI: 10.1177/1745691610369336

12   Schmitt, Bernd. 2012. "The consumer psychology of brands". *Journal of Consumer Psychology*, 22(1): 7-17.
     DOI: https://doi.org/10.1016/j.jcps.2011.09.005

13   Aaker, Jennifer L., Benet-Martinez, Veronica. and Garolera, Jordi. 2001. "Consumption symbols as carriers of culture: A study of Japanese and Spanish brand personality constructs". *Journal of personality and social psychology*, 81(3), 492.508
     DOI: 10.1037/0022-3514.81.3.492

14   Park, Ji K., and John, D. R. 2010. "Got to get you into my life: Do brand personalities rub off on consumers?" *Journal of Consumer Research*, 37(4): 655–669.

DOI: 10.1086/655807

15 Batra, R., Ahuvia, A., and Bagozzi, R. P. 2012. Brand love. *Journal of Marketing*, 76(2), 1–16.
    DOI: https://doi.org/10.1509/jm.09.0339

16 Park, Whan., Eisingerich, Andreas B. and Park, Jason W. 2013. "Attachment–aversion (AA) model of customer–brand relationships". *Journal of Consumer Psychology*, 23(2),229–48.
    DOI: https://doi.org/10.1016/j.jcps.2013.01.002

17 Aaker, Jennifer L. 1997. "Dimensions of brand personality". *Journal of Marketing Research*, 34(3): 347–56.
    DOI: https://doi.org/10.1177/002224379703400304

18 Geuens, Maggie., Weijters, Bert. and De Wulf, Kristof. 2009. "A new measure of brand personality". *International Journal of Research in Marketing*, 26(2): 97–107.
    DOI: https://doi.org/10.1016/j.ijresmar.2008.12.002

19 Avis, Mark., Forbes, Sarah., and Ferguson, Shelagh. 2014. "The brand personality of rocks: A critical evaluation of a brand personality scale". *Marketing Theory*, 14(4): 451-475.
    DOI: https://doi.org/10.1177/1470593113512323

20 Rauschnabel, Philipp., Krey, Nina., Babin, Barry J. and Ivens, Bjoern S. 2016. "Brand management in higher education: the university brand personality scale". *Journal of Business Research*, 69(8): 3077–86.
    DOI: https://doi.org/10.1016/j.jbusres.2016.01.023

21 Freling, Traci H., Crosno, Jody. L., and Henard, David. H. 2011. "Brand personality appeal: conceptualization and empirical validation". *Journal of the Academy of Marketing Science*, 39(3): 392–406.
    DOI: https://doi.org/10.1007/s11747-010-0208-3

22 Malone, Chris. and Fiske, Susan. T. *The human brand: How we relate to people, products, and companies.* (John Wiley & Sons. 2013).

5

From Social Responsibility to Woke Activism

The era of having a corporate social responsibility (CSR) department that does all the good things while the rest of the organization continues doing all the bad things are numbered. For many years companies have used CSR as a mechanism to soften their commercial image (an image that overemphasizes profit and revenue).

In recent years, companies have realized they need a more compelling social responsibility strategy and one that expands beyond the CSR department. More and more brands are coming to the conclusion that choosing a safe and simple cause to sponsor or choosing a safe nonprofit partner to collaborate with and sponsor isn't going to impress their target audience. Taking a lazy, donation-focused approach to social responsibility and just touching the surface isn't going to cut it anymore.

Instead, brands are moving toward translating their social responsibilities into their internal and external actions throughout the organization, in all departments. Embracing the concept of purposefulness, brands are building on humane values and are practicing being good corporate citizens in all aspects of their business. That includes responsible pricing, ethical advertising, sustainable products, fair treatment of employees, celebrating diversity, inclusion and equality, and being transparent. Ethical behavior doesn't need to be and shouldn't be limited to certain parts; it needs to be practiced in all departments across the organization.

Purposeful brands, such as Dove and Chobani focus on walking the talk. They show accountability and commitment toward social issues by empowering their target audience and employees to find the better version of themselves.

Often a long-term strategy, brand purpose is a slow-cooked and patient approach toward building a responsible, accountable, and committed brand. A purposeful brand applies humane values in all different business practices and integrates them into the organization's culture.

There are, however, brands that have taken purposefulness to another level, getting woke and championing controversial social and political issues often linked to trendy social movements, such as BLM and MeToo. Brands with a woke activism mindset parachute into high-tension and sensitive sociopolitical issues that are either relevant to the target audience or important to society.

The Journey Towards Woke From CSR

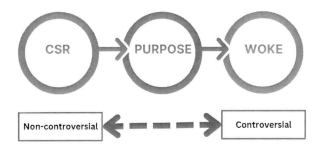

The Journey toward Woke from CSR

CSR can be defined as international private business self-regulation.[1] CSR can be viewed from different perspectives, such as social, economic, stakeholder, and voluntary.[2] CSR is about designing "policies and practices of corporations that reflect business responsibility for some of the wider societal good."[3]

CSR initiatives are different from purposeful and woke campaigns. CSR campaigns are not controversial in nature. They are rarely partisan, and there is greater agreement among the public about CSR actions and outcomes. CSR initiatives are not necessarily directly and significantly aligned with an organization's internal practices. They are not necessarily holistic, representing the entire organization's practices. Instead, they are a sideshow, conforming to the brand public's minimum expectations.

Finally, CSR practices are based on philanthropy and are heavily involved with charitable activities and donations.

Table 1 provides a comparison of CSR, purpose, and woke initiatives, across a range of factors.

Table 1: How CSR, Purpose, and Woke Initiatives Differ

	CSR	Purposeful	Woke
Controversy	Low	Low to Medium	High
Dividing (partisan)	Low	Low to Medium	High
Response Homogeneity	High	Medium to High	Low
Expectation	Low	Medium	High
Practice Alignment	Low	High	Low to High
Brand personality/ positioning	Conforming (Not a personality or image/ positioning)	To build personality and form positioning	To build personality and form positioning
	Short-term	Long-term	Long-term

From CSR to Purpose

As described above and shown in Table 1, CSR initiatives are limited and mostly surface level, conforming to the brand public's basic expectations regarding a business's role in the society as an agent of change. Thus, recently there have been calls for businesses to go beyond just having good intentions and for them to try to provide purposeful solutions to solve social and environmental issues.[4]

In line with this call, the demonstration of corporate social accountability has gone beyond CSR and is being reflected in corporate purpose—that is, building organizations that practice humane values, such as achievement, empowerment, benevolence, security, and self-direction. Brand purpose can provide an umbrella framework for examining the role of a business in society.[5] Commitment to diversity, reducing violence toward women and empowering them, or supporting child adoption rights for transgender people are among the social purposes embraced by brands such as Airbnb, Vicks, and Tecate.[6]

Purpose is the essence of the brand[9]. Purpose is what a brand stands for. It's the reason the brand exists beyond making a profit. Tightly linking brand purpose to an organization's culture and values[7] is one way to attract and connect with consumers. Standing for a higher purpose can become a competitive advantage and a driver of future growth.[6] Purposeful branding has a holistic and inclusive view toward social responsibility and accountability. Compared to CSR, purposefulness requires a long-term commitment toward practicing and delivering on the purpose promise.

Brands such as Dove, Chobani, and Patagonia did not gain their respected positioning overnight. Instead, that positioning has been the outcome of years of commitment toward celebrating humane values in everyday business, including self-enhancement, openness to change, and conservation.

However, CSR and purposeful practices have one thing in common, and that is adopting less controversial causes. That is the point of difference between CSR and purposefulness versus wokeness. Woke is controversial by nature. In its DNA, woke is partisan. It directly targets hot-button social and political issues and questions the status quo.

Case Study: Chobani

Brands can take two routes toward activism. Some brands take the route of slow-cooked, patient activism, employing strategies in line with their brand purpose without heavily featuring and showing off such activities in their marketing campaigns.

Chobani provides an example of this type of patient and purposeful activism. By implementing a profit-sharing model with employees, hiring and supporting asylum seekers, and funding start-ups through the Chobani Foundation and Chobani incubator, Chobani has gone well beyond selling yogurt and adopted a higher purpose.[8] Chobani has taken a less controversial and slightly silent brand activism approach by not leveraging its key purposeful moves through the integration of these moves in its mainstream communications with the target audience.

An alternative route toward actioning brand purpose strategies is to publicly advocate and communicate a brand's purpose, a public virtue-signaling attempt, thus trying to influence the target audience's attitudes and behaviors toward the brand. Brand purpose is in this setting a key building block of brand activism.

From Purpose to Woke

Getting woke—and demonstrating wokeness through corporate social advocacy (CSA) and corporate political advocacy (CPA)—entails becoming aware of social issues and using corporate resources to fight injustice, inequality, and prejudice.

CSR is mostly associated with less controversial causes where there is a social consensus (that is, it concerns itself with pro-social issues that aren't divisive, such as supporting children's education). But woke is built on controversial issues and involves taking a definitive stance on those divisive issues, inevitably generating positive and negative responses (or sometimes just overwhelmingly negative responses).

In woke activism initiatives, there is less social consensus and therefore greater division in how the public interprets the woke message and intentions. This is mainly because there is no single "right way" for brands to address social and political issues. Therefore, woke activism can be seen as a significant evolution of CSR.

Woke is the meaning brands try to communicate by employing and executing different strategies. Once the woke title is owned, brands have no choice but to constantly demonstrate they are woke. A brand can be an advocate for a social, political, or an environmental issue without being woke. Conforming to the norms and meeting the expectations of the target audience can suffice to win the CSR badge.

In contrast, a woke brand is expected to be the leader, pioneer, and frontrunner in the fight against injustice and to always adopt a higher purpose.

References

1   Sheehy, Benedict., 2015. "Defining CSR: Problems and solutions". *Journal of Business Ethics*, *131*(3), 625–48.
    DOI: https://doi.org/10.1007/s10551-014-2281-x
2   Dahlsrud, Alexander., 2008. "How corporate social responsibility is defined: an analysis of 37 definitions". *Corporate Social Responsibility and Environmental Management*, *15*(1), 1–13.
    DOI: https://doi.org/10.1002/csr.132
3   Matten, Dirk. and Moon, Jeremy., 2008. "Implicit" and "explicit" CSR: A conceptual framework for a comparative understanding of corporate social responsibility". *Academy of management Review*, *33*(2), 404–24.
    DOI: 10.5465/AMR.2008.31193458

4   Barnett, Michael L., Henriques, Irene. and Husted, Bryan W., 2020. "Beyond good intentions: Designing CSR initiatives for greater social impact". *Journal of Management*, *46*(6), 937–64. DOI: https://doi.org/10.1177/0149206319900539

5   Hollensbe, E., Wookey, C., Hickey, L., George, G. and Nichols, C.V., 2014. "Organizations with purpose". *Academy of Management Journal*, *57*(5), 1227–34.

6   Vilá, O.R. and Bharadwaj, S., 2017. "Competing on social purpose: Brands that win by tying mission to growth." *Harvard Business Review.*

7   Greyser, S.A. and Urde, M., 2019. "What does your corporate brand stand for". *Harvard Business Review, 1*(2), 82–89.

8   Mainwaring, Simon. Purpose at work: How Chobani builds a purposeful culture around social impact. Forbes, August 27, 2018. https://www.forbes.com/sites/simonmainwaring/2018/08/27/how-chobani-builds-a-purposeful-culture-around-social-impact/?sh=1e793dab20f7.

9   Mirzaei, Abas, Cynthia M. Webster, and Helen Siuki. (2021). "Exploring brand purpose dimensions for non-profit organizations." Journal of Brand Management 28, no. 2: 186-198. https://doi.org/10.1057/s41262-020-00224-4

6

Woke Consumers

Over the past few years there has been a considerable shift among consumers toward expressing how conscious they are about their environment, whether it is their social, environmental, nature-based, legal, or political environment.[1]

Consumers are moving toward buying meaning, purpose, and a certain mindset, rather than just a functional benefit. Consumers may even go beyond brand personalities and ask themselves and the brand, what else do you have to offer on humane values, besides a cool, rugged, or sophisticated personality?

A socially conscious consumer might believe his or her choice of products and services is a positive social act when buying from a brand the consumer believes embodies the right values. Often labelled as woke, consumers concerned with social injustice have become proactive, calling out those businesses and brands that are not doing their fair share in fighting issues such as racism, sexism, and ageism.

The woke consumer has become a public activist, contributing to callout culture and, in extreme cases, cancel culture. A brand's mistakes can be tolerated no longer; woke activist consumers will use social media platforms to call out the brand and publicly pressure it to help change the status quo. Consumers are increasingly supporting their beliefs with their purchase decisions, backing those brands aligned with their values and avoiding those that are not.[2]

Up to a reported third of consumers globally are making purchase decisions influenced by a higher purpose and principal values.[2] In particular, the younger generations of consumers show greater interest in brands that show a commitment to addressing social issues and supporting campaigns such as #MeToo, #TimesUp and #BLM.[2]

According to global research conducted by Accenture in 2019, [3] 62 percent of customers expect companies to take a stand on social issues. If companies do not do this, they are likely to pay the price, with 53 percent of consumers likely to complain if they are unhappy with the brand's words or actions, while 47 percent will switch to other brands. Research carried out by Edelman in

2020 shows that if consumers trust the brand on social issues, not only will they buy the brand, seven out of ten will advocate for and defend the brand.[4]

Research by WARC [5] in 2020 also shows that consumers have added elements other than product quality into their trust equation. This means brands need to deliver on other factors that are less objective and tangible but more crucial in trust building and purchase decision.

Consumers are demanding brands to use their power to drive change in society, creating a better world that is more diverse for everyone [6] and educating the public about issues such as racial inequality.[7]

However, woke consumers won't easily trust brands that claim they're committed to social issues, perceiving it as *woke washing* (aka *trust washing*).[5] More than half of customers surveyed were skeptical of brands' involvement in social issues, arguing brands have profit-seeking motivations.[5] Unless the promise is backed by authentic action, the race to reflect societal values can lead to consumer backlash.[6]

Consumers may be motivated to signal they are woke due to other related socio-political factors. Ulver and Laurell put consumer activists into four categories: anticapitalist, anticolonialist, antiunethical, and antiexclusionist.[8]

Consumer Activist Categories

Anticapitalists focus on the entire economic system, including anticonsumerism. In this category, the real capitalism and unreflective users are the main adversaries.

Anticolonialist are tied to religious and nationalist ideologies. For instance, how Islamism can inform brand meanings,[9] where activists may encourage consumers from using Western brands, labelling them as *haram*. Activists in this category focus on resisting geopolitical capitalism.[8]

Antiunethicals are triggered to call out brands when they perceive business misconduct, labelling such brand practices as corrupt and psychopathic.[8] Previous research finds that antiunethical activist consumers tend to collaborate with not-for-profit cause-marketing organizations in an attempt to inspire and encourage ethical consumption among the public.[10] Overall, this type of activist consumerism focuses on forcing businesses to act ethically.[11, 12]

Antiexclusionists question and fight discrimination. Consumers in this category have often been the victim of discrimination themselves, which motivates them to push for a change in the status quo.[8] Plus-size fashion consumers [13] and Minamoto bikers are among the examples of consumer activists who have called for more inclusive business practices.[14]

Woke consumers mostly fall into the antiunethical and antiexclusion categories of consumer activists and are committed to fighting discrimination and unethical business practices. Woke consumers push for more inclusion and diversity in business practices. Moreover, woke consumers expect and encourage businesses to go beyond standard business practices and invest in the fight against discrimination, actively advocate for inclusive values and take a stand on important social and political issues that may have disadvantaged some communities.

Woke consumers also fight the antiliberal and anti-progressive consumers. They resist those consumers who resist multiculturalism and diversity. Antiliberals are personified as consumers who hold strong nationalist values and view anyone they perceive as challenging national interests as the enemy.[8]

Euromonitor's Global Consumer Type report, which is based on the Voice of Consumer Survey, classifies consumers into ten different groups such as:

1. empowered activist;
2. impulsive spender;
3. minimalist seeker; and
4. balanced optimist.

In particular, empowered activists are those consumers who value environmentalism and progressive sociopolitical values and who believe they have the power to affect change. Empowered activists' numbers are on the rise, increasing from 9 percent in 2019 to 15 percent in 2021. Empowered activist consumers, who are usually loyal customers, are vocal in expressing their values and often expect the companies they purchase from to share these values.[15]

Consumer Types

I offer four types of consumers based on the degree of their wokeness:

- functionality seeker;
- purposeful consumer;
- woke; and
- personality alignment driven (PAD).

Functionality Seeker

Until recently, brands were focused on two types of consumers, and most of their branding decisions were around impressing these two key groups. The first type of consumer is unemotional and just expects a product to get the job done. A functionality seeker's interaction with a barista might go something like this.

> **Functionality Seeker:** "I need a coffee. It can be strong, it can be with milk, it can have sugar or no sugar. But don't ask me how I feel about the message on the cup, don't tell me how the coffee bean farmers are faring, don't tell me what charity you're donating one cent per cup of coffee to. Plus, I don't care if the cup is recyclable or not. I'm late for work, I feel sleepy, and my brain won't function without a coffee. Can you help me, dear barista?"
> **Barista:** "Sounds like you need a strong long black, with no sugar, take away."
> **Functionality Seeker:** "Correct!"

Personality Alignment Driven (PAD)

The last group of consumers see brands as entities that they can develop feelings for and treat like pets. As mentioned in chapter 3, according to implicit self-theory, consumers are two types: entity theorist and incremental theorist.

Entity Theorists

This group of consumers believe their personality is fixed, and they should rely on objects, such as brands, to improve their personality and cover the gap between their actual personality and the desired personality.

Incremental Theorists

This group of consumers believe their personality is malleable and can be improved through their own efforts.

Entity theorist consumers want to go beyond functionality and look for abstract emotion-based benefits. Brand personality, brand mindset, image, and character play a major role in their choice of brand and their brand relationship. The higher the degree of connection between a brand's personality and a consumer's actual or desired self and social self, the more valuable the brand is in that consumer's mind. For these consumers, the choice of coffee should also tell the world a little about the user and their profile, lifestyle, social class, and desired personality. Put simply, for this group, not only product features but also brand attributes are important.

From a branding perspective, this type of consumer can be preferable. This is because the challenge with the Functionality Seeker consumer, from a brand viewpoint, is that the brand offering could be easily copied and thus neutralized by competitors. Competing on functional benefits means brands are always vulnerable to losing consumers to alternative and substitute offerings.

What can we add to our offerings that will make us more protected and less at risk of being challenged by a better-tangible offering? Well, let's add a bit of something invisible, which consumers can't see, can't describe, can't deny, and can't argue about: emotion, an intangible ingredient that will target feelings and trigger an emotional response. What's the best way to trigger human emotion? To communicate a humanlike characteristic, mindset, and personality. This can be done by investing heavily in branding. By designing and crafting logos, taglines, characters, and personalities that signal the type of personality consumers are looking for.

So for the personality alignment driven consumer, a coffee that wakes them up (gets the job done) is not enough. The message on the cup is also important. Likewise, the background music playing, the uniforms the café staff are wearing, the friendliness of the barista, and other sensory elements of the experience are also important.

Purposeful Consumer

This group of consumers not only want a coffee that gets the job done and is aligned with their personality and image, they are open to conversations about the fate of coffee growers and are interested in knowing how the brand is treating its employees.

Built on the collective-thinking principle, purposeful consumers don't just focus on themselves in their purchase decisions and brand choices. They care about others and the impact of their decisions on the wider society and the environment. These consumers are interested in the behind-the-scenes practices of brands as much as their publicly visible practices.

For many years, Nespresso ran the What Else? campaign featuring George Clooney to communicate a personality of elegance, style, and sophistication. But purposeful consumers questioned Nespresso's poor treatment of coffee farmers. This ultimately resulted in the launch of a new campaign: The Choices We Make.

Purposeful consumers can have similarities to functionality seekers or personality alignment driven consumers. However, they are prepared to make a suboptimal purchase decision, compromising on quality, performance, experience, or personality alignment when competing brands don't deliver on higher-order human values.

For instance, even if the Nike Air shoes are comfortable and durable, even if I love Nike, and its brand personality represents me and who I want to be and what I want to communicate to the world, I might decide against buying Nike's shoes. I might go with Allbirds instead if I believe they treat their employees and subcontractors better and have never been associated with sweatshops.

Woke Consumer

Woke consumers are more critical than purposeful consumers. They have had enough of the "Blah, blah, blah" (to borrow from young activist Greta Thunberg's speech at the UN Climate Conference, COP26) they typically get from brands.

Woke consumers want brands to make brave moves and address hot-button sociopolitical issues, rather than just safe purposeful issues. Woke consumers prioritize humane values over functionality and quality and see a commitment to solving major social issues as more a "must" move for brands rather than a cute move.

While a yogurt brand looking after employees and sharing the wealth with them is purposeful (Chobani), woke consumers expect the yogurt brand to also address highly charged issues around discrimination and injustice.

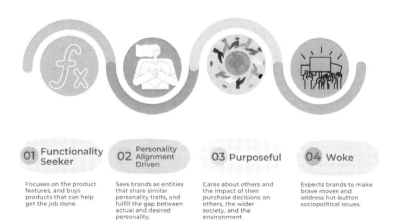

From Functionality Seeker to Woke Consumer

01 Functionality Seeker

Focuses on the product features, and buys products that can help get the job done.

02 Personality Alignment Driven

Sees brands as entities that share similar personality traits, and fulfill the gap between actual and desired personality.

03 Purposeful

Cares about others and the impact of their purchase decisions on others, the wider society, and the environment.

04 Woke

Expects brands to make brave moves and address hot-button sociopolitical issues.

From Functionality Seeker to Woke Consumers in the Coffee Industry

For years, Folgers [16] has focused on emotional appeal—"the best part of waking up every morning"—neglecting the product and its quality. In a recent campaign launched in January 2022, the top-selling coffee brand in the US market has been trying to reintroduce itself, to stop losing more customers to other coffee brands.

Providing comments to AdAge,[16] Erica Roberts, chief creative officer of Publicis New York (the ad agency behind the campaign), highlights the change in Folgers' messaging: "We've always talked about the best part of waking up, but we never talked about the best parts of the best parts of waking up. That's things like what goes into the coffee itself, [and] how it's made …"

Another pain point contributing to losing customers emerging from the brand's market research was associated with the lack of personality alignment. Many consumers thought the brand wasn't for them, as the brand image was perceived as "Grandma's choice," limiting the expansion to other coffee drinker personas.

To address this, the brand has launched four episodes of a reintroducing campaign: "Think of us as your grandma's coffee? Heck, yes we are—and thirty-five million more with equally excellent taste." The campaign features a range of different age groups, personas, and usage situations, trying to appeal to different target audience who may resonate with the brand.

Other coffee brands, like Nespresso, have gone another step up the ladder, from focusing heavily on personality alignment and brand image to purposeful messaging (especially following reports [17] of child labor in its supply chain in the Fraijanes region of Guatemala). With messages like "When coffee has the power to transform communities," Nespresso realized it was time to switch from its dated What Else? campaign to more purposeful communications and practices highlighting the effect of consumer choices and brand practices on farmers and their communities.

Starbucks, the street corner coffee brand, once attempted to leapfrog purposefulness and appeal to woke consumers, launching its now infamous Race Together campaign. The brand parachuted into the race discrimination and injustice issue without considering their existing image, their customer base, and the public's perceptions of the brand, surprising the audience. Coupled with its poor execution and rushed approach in solving the deep sociopolitical issues, the campaign was soon pulled and an apology issued.

References

1   Alemany, Christine. Marketing in the age of resistance. *Harvard Business Review.* September 3, 2020. https://hbr.org/2020/09/marketing-in-the-age-of-resistance.

2   Amed, Imran., Balchandani, Anita., Beltrami, Marco., Berg, Achim., Hedrich, Saskia., and Rölkens, Felix. (2019). The influence of "woke" consumers on fashion. *MacKinsey and Company.* https://www.mckinsey.com/industries/retail/our-insights/the-influence-of-woke-consumers-on-fashion.

3   Accenture. (2019). *To affinity and beyond: From me to we, the rise of the purpose-led brand.* https://www.accenture.com/_acnmedia/thought-leadership-assets/pdf/accenture-competitiveagility-gcpr-pov.pdf.

4   Edelman. (2020). *Edelman trust barometer.* http://www.edelman.de/research/edelman-trust-barometer-2020.

5   WARC. (2021). What we know about brand purpose.

https://www-warc-com.simsrad.net.ocs.mq.edu.au/content/article/bestprac/what-we-know-about-brand-purpose/109945.

6   Bakhtiari, Kian. (2020). *Why brands need to pay attention to cancel culture.* Forbes. https://www.forbes.com/sites/kianbakhtiari/2020/09/29/why-brands-need-to-pay-attention-to-cancel-culture/?sh=4ad464fe645e.

7   Menon, Geeta., and Kiesler, Tina. (2020). When a brand stands up for racial justice, do people buy it?. *Harvard Business Review.* https://hbr.org/2020/07/when-a-brand-stands-up-for-racial-justice-do-people-buy-it.

8   Ulver-Sneistrup, Sofia. and Laurell, Christofer. (2020). "Political ideology in consumer resistance: Analyzing far-right opposition to multicultural marketing". *Journal of public policy and marketing, 39*(4), 477–93. DOI: https://doi.org/10.1177/0743915620947083

9   Izberk-Bilgin, Elif. (2012). "Infidel brands: Unveiling alternative meanings of global brands at the nexus of globalization, consumer culture, and Islamism". *Journal of Consumer Research, 39*(4), 663–687. DOI: https://doi.org/10.1086/665413

10   Gopaldas, Ahir. (2014). Marketplace sentiments. *Journal of Consumer Research, 41*(4), 995–1014. DOI: https://doi.org/10.1086/678034

11   Ulver-Sneistrup, Sofia., Askegaard, Soren., and Kristensen, Dorthe B., (2011). "The new work ethics of consumption and the paradox of mundane brand resistance". *Journal of Consumer Culture, 11*(2), 215–38. DOI: https://doi.org/10.1177/1469540511402447

12   Thompson, Craig J., and Kumar, Ankita. (2021). Beyond consumer responsibilization: Slow Food's actually existing neoliberalism. *Journal of Consumer Culture, 21*(2), 317–36. DOI: https://doi.org/10.1177/1469540518818632

13   Scaraboto, Daiane. and Fischer, Eileen. (2013). Frustrated fatshionistas: An institutional theory perspective on consumer quests for greater choice in mainstream markets. *Journal of Consumer Research, 39*(6), 1234–57. DOI: https://doi.org/10.1086/668298

14   Martin, Diane M. and Schouten, John W. (2014). Consumption-driven market emergence. *Journal of consumer research, 40*(5), 855–70. DOI: https://doi.org/10.1086/673196

15 *Euromonitor.* Understanding the Path to Purchase: 2021 Global Consumer Types, https://go.euromonitor.com/white-paper-consumers-210518-global-consumer-types.html.

16 Springer, John. Inside Folgers' Effort to Embrace Its "Bad Reputation," *AdAge,* January 31, 2022. https://adage.com/article/marketing-news-strategy/folgers-new-campaign-embraces-its-reputation/2396016.

17 Brown, Nick. Nespresso Releases Plan to Combat Child Labor Found in its Supply Chain, *Daily Coffee News,* April 7, 2020, https://dailycoffeenews.com/2020/04/07/nespresso-releases-plan-to-combat-child-labor-found-in-its-supply-chain/.

7

Woke Activism Authenticity

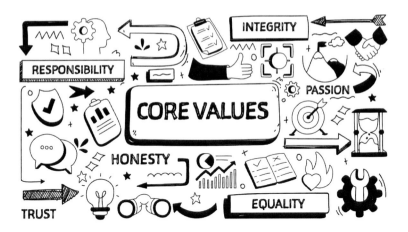

Imagine you walk into a Thai restaurant to have your favorite dish, green curry. While you see all the Thai food items on the menu, something about the place doesn't seem right. Those cues and elements you have in mind about a Thai restaurant are not to be found. The waiters don't look Thai, their uniforms are not in the traditional Thai style, the decorations don't remind you of your trip to Thailand, and even the chef is not Thai.

You're confused, because while you love the food and enjoy the overall restaurant experience, you feel something is missing. You don't feel you've walked into a Thai restaurant, since you didn't see any of the elements you expected. While you had a great experience, it hasn't been an authentic Thai experience.

Authenticity has been defined and evaluated with different lenses. Indexical authenticity, iconic authenticity, authenticity as proximity to the creator, being true to self, conformity, consistency, or connection are some of the different lenses used to perceive authenticity.

To investigate why people have different and sometimes inconsistent perceptions of authenticity in different contexts, Professor Balázs Kovács from Yale University conducted a bottom-up exploratory survey in which participants listed the words they associate with authentic restaurants, people, paintings, brands, and organizations.

Authenticity in the Context of Woke Activism

Given the growing interest in woke communications, brands are moving toward embedding social and political issues in their advertising campaigns and taking a stance and addressing major issues. Brands are signaling they are woke. The corporate world is taking a proactive stance in the way it is responding to issues such as racism and sexism. By transitioning toward woke communications, household brands are going beyond the functional benefits of their products.

In an era of movements, such as MeToo and Black Lives Matter, brands are motivated to become social justice warriors and are showing an appetite to tackle complex issues.

However, the lack of experience and expertise in understanding how the target audience is decoding their carefully coded woke message can turn a brand's promising (on paper) campaign, portraying a more meaningful and compassionate image into a short-lived, backlash-generating public relations disaster.

Wokeness is unfamiliar territory for brands and involves both opportunities and risks. Woke communications come with the risk of mixed responses—from woke praising to woke shaming; from "buycott" to boycott; and from a spike in sales and share prices to a brand value write-off. [1]

This suggests that target audiences have their own criteria to evaluate brands' woke moves, and convincing consumers that brands genuinely have the interests of the public at heart when drifting toward wokeness has appeared to be a hard sell.

The higher the degree of perceived woke authenticity, the greater the degree of woke praising, and the lesser the degree of woke shaming, and vice versa. With many consumers questioning the true motivations of brands becoming woke and accusing them of corrupt, profit-oriented motivations, and inauthentic virtue signaling, it is crucial to understand the factors contributing toward lack of perceived authenticity in woke communications. This chapter proposes that authenticity is the primary driver of whether brands experience woke praising or woke shaming.

Authenticity Conceptualization

Tackling sensitive social issues may seem to contradict the ultimate goal of commercial brands: profit-seeking. When it has no apparent connection to deep-rooted injustices in the society, a brand's involvement in social issues may seem a surface-level attempt.

This contradiction between the perceived purpose of a brand (profit seeking) and woke higher-purpose values, communicated and signaled, has been a significant obstacle toward society's acceptance of brands' engagement in tackling social issues.

Despite brands' involvement in consumers' daily lives, consumers seem not to welcome what brands have to offer when it comes to sensitive issues. This can be a major lost opportunity for both parties. Brands with their power in terms of financial support, product development, communication and public awareness, audience reach, and employment practices can be an impactful agent of change. It is also a lost opportunity for brands to develop a long-term relationship with, and becoming and staying relevant to, their target audience.

One way of overcoming such obstacles is to facilitate consumer acceptance of brands' virtue signaling attempts by assuring them of the authenticity of such attempts. Convincing the consumer that the brands' moves are genuine and authentic, and their motivations are not corrupt, can turn a lose-lose scenario into a win-win one.

Two Views toward Authenticity

The existing literature on authenticity in marketing can be discussed from consumer versus brand perspectives. [2] Consumer-related authenticity captures consumer experience in forms of indexical (suggesting the originality of the object) [3] and iconic cues (constructed by marketers to resemble the real thing). [2,4] Brand-related authenticity can be divided into three main categories: general brand authenticity, advertising authenticity, and corporate social responsibility (CSR) authenticity.

General brand authenticity is mostly focused on dimensions such as expertise, heritage, and conforming to what is expected.

A brand's past, cultural fit,[5] heritage, sincerity,[6] symbolism, and continuity[7] are examples of general brand authenticity dimensions. This view has a direct link to the brand and its products.

However, the advertising authenticity perspective has a more specific communication-related focus toward authenticity. It focuses on how different themes of advertising can be perceived as authentic. Becker and colleagues, for instance, propose themes such as realistic plot and advertising credibility as dimensions of advertising authenticity.[2] Shoenberger et al. note that authenticity in advertising, which can be manifested in an authentic experience or an authentic spokesperson, can have a positive effect on consumers' purchase decisions. In their study, they suggest being real (about Instagram ad models) is a key driver of being perceived as authentic.

Overall, the previous literature has proposed a variety of dimensions for authenticity, from connection to history and heritage, to virtuousness, sincerity, and commitment. Historical authenticity happens when people evaluate the authenticity of an object by examining its history and connection to a valued entity such as person, place, or event.[9] Historical authenticity can come in different forms, including indexical, nominal, and pure authenticity.[9, 10] Referral authenticity[11] captures aspects such as heritage, history, and connectedness, which connect the brand to its cultural associations.[12]

In the context of social responsibility, brands signaling they're committed to taking responsibility for social issues are expected to show the connection between their initiative and the community's concern.[13, 14]

Brand authenticity can also be achieved through signaling sincerity, identity, and virtuousness. Communicating values that consumers can relate to and, more importantly, use to define who they are can contribute toward authentic brand perception by fulfilling one's desired self and social values.[7] This dimension resonates with virtuousness (staying true to your moral values),[15] and value authenticity, which is conceptualized as the extent to which there is a synergy between an entity's internal states and external expressions.[9] This is also referred to as expressive authenticity [16] or moral authenticity.[17] The synchronicity and synergy between what is communicated and what the internal estate can become is a crucial aspect of authentic woke communications. This is because it highlights the degree of overlap between what a brand does in reality and what the brand is symbolically signaling. This suggests that being perceived as transparent, honest, and committed [6] can contribute to the perception of authenticity.

A lack of synchronicity between what a brand does and what it communicates and advocates for can signal the brand is exaggerating and looking for trendy topics to signal values that are important for its target audience. Such perception may negatively affect the brand authenticity.[14]

Woke Authenticity Conceptualization

Prior research has provided a list of authenticity dimensions. But the applicability of these authenticity dimensions to a situation involving brand public's concerns—be they political, social, or legal—is questionable.

Woke campaigns leverage controversial issues where the public is divided. They reference hot-button topics and involve consciously wading into controversy. Consumers ruthlessly evaluate brands' woke authenticity, as evidenced by the social media comments brands such as Gillette, Amazon, or Pepsi have received about their woke communications.

"Your pandering virtue signaling and lecturing on toxic masculinity is disingenuous."

"Stay in your lane."

"Such a real and authentic message. We can all do better! [It] should be the parents' job, not some billion-dollar company that only care about profits."

"Wonder how genuine this advertising campaign is?"

Comments like these highlight the mixed response woke campaigns have received in the past.

I propose five dimensions to woke authenticity. The woke authenticity dimensions give brands a comprehensive perspective on the road toward woke authenticity[18]. It will enable brands to have a better understanding of the dynamics of woke authenticity perceptions by the public. This will give brands a greater ability to convince the public of the genuine motivations behind woke communications and get the support of the public, reducing the risk of consumer backlash.

- Motivation;
- Alignment;
- Practice;
- History;
- Inclusion & Diversity

Motivation

The perceived motivations behind corporates' engagement in social issues can influence judgments on woke authenticity. Not-for-profit organizations' motivations are less at risk of being perceived as inauthentic. But commercial and for-profit brands' social engagements are always at risk of being labelled as corrupt and financially oriented.

There is a widespread belief that commercial brands only engage in pro-social initiatives if there is a financial benefit for them. Thus, their motivations can be easily perceived as corrupt and profit-seeking. Consequently, the target audience observes and digests woke activism gestures through the lens of cynicism.

Alignment

The degree of alignment between the brand's core business, its image and positioning, and the woke issue can influence perceived woke authenticity. Any misalignment may risk backlash and potential boycotting, whereas a high degree of alignment is likely to increase perceptions of genuineness. To be perceived as authentic, an organization's social responsibility program should be strongly associated with its core values and culture.

Practice

Another important factor when judging the authenticity of a brand is the extent to which the brand is living up to, and is committed to delivering, what it promises.[6] Whether the brand is walking the talk and is showing commitment toward tackling the issue they are getting woke for is an essential factor in evaluating the authenticity of the brand's woke activist move.

History

If the brand has a history of engaging in activism and higher purpose moves, and if the brand is known for championing social and political issues, woke authenticity may be perceived differently by the brand public. Brands that don't have any history of being purposeful and which abruptly get involved in wokeness may confuse the brand public. They are likely to query why a previously apolitical brand is now representing itself as a social justice warrior. Having a relevant preexisting history and positioning can facilitate the brand public's understanding and decoding of woke authenticity.

Inclusion and Diversity

While there is a growing expectation that brands should not remain silent on social issues, taking a stand on a social issue and supporting a disadvantaged group can be perceived by some as discrimination against other groups. Brands focusing too narrowly on a social issue risk being exclusive and thus risk a backlash from those who feel left out. A brand's message should be inclusive even when highlighting the discrimination suffered by a particular group.

References

1   Naidu, Richa., and Soundarya, J. *P&G posts strong sales, takes $8 billion Gillette writedown*. Reuters. July 30, 2019. https://de.reuters.com/article/us-proctergamble-results/pg-posts-strong-profit-amid-8-billion-writedown-of-gillette-idUKKCN1UP1AD

2   Becker, Maren., Wiegand, Nico., and Reinartz, Werner J. (2019). "Does it pay to be real? Understanding authenticity in TV advertising". *Journal of Marketing, 83*(1), 24–50. DOI: https://doi.org/10.1177/0022242918815880

3   Allen, Chris T. Ewing, Douglas L., and Ewing, Randall L., (2012). "Authenticity as meaning validation: An empirical investigation of iconic and indexical cues in a context of "green" products". *Journal of Consumer Behavior, 11*(5), 381–90.

4   Grayson, Kent. and Martinec, Radan., (2004). "Consumer perceptions of iconicity and indexicality and their influence on assessments of authentic market offerings". *Journal of consumer research, 31*(2), 296-312. DOI: https://doi.org/10.1086/422109

5   Fritz, Kristine., Schoenmueller, Verena., and Bruhn, Manfred. (2017). "Authenticity in branding-exploring antecedents and consequences of brand authenticity". *European Journal of Marketing, 51*(2), 324–348. DOI: https://doi.org/10.1108/EJM-10-2014-0633

6   Napoli, Julie., Dickinson, Sonia J., Beverland, Michael B., and Farrelly, Francis. (2014). "Measuring consumer-based brand authenticity". *Journal of Business Research*, *67*(6), 1090–1098.
DOI: https://doi.org/10.1016/j.jbusres.2013.06.001

7   Morhart, Felicitas., Malär, Lucia., Guèvremont, Amelie., Girardin, Florent., and Grohmann, Bianca. (2015). "Brand authenticity: An integrative framework and measurement scale". *Journal of Consumer Psychology*, *25*(2), 200–18.
DOI: https://doi.org/10.1016/j.jcps.2014.11.006

8   Shoenberger, Heather., Kim, Eujin. and Johnson, Erika K., (2020). "Role of Perceived Authenticity of Digital Enhancement of Model Advertising Images on Brand Attitudes, Social Media Engagement". *Journal of Interactive Advertising*, *20*(3), 181-195.
DOI: https://doi.org/10.1080/15252019.2020.1840459

9   Newman, George E. (2019). "The psychology of authenticity". *Review of General Psychology*, *23*(1), 8–18.
DOI: https://doi.org/10.1037/gpr0000158

10 Newman, George. E., and Smith, Rosana K. (2016). Kinds of authenticity. *Philosophy Compass*, *11*(10), 609–618.
DOI: https://doi.org/10.1111/phc3.12343

11 Pine, Joseph B., and Gilmore, James H., (2007). *Authenticity: What consumers really want*. Harvard Business Press.

12 Spiggle, Susan., Nguyen, Hang. T., and Caravella, Mary. (2012). "More than fit: Brand extension authenticity". *Journal of Marketing Research*, *49(6)*, 967–983.
DOI: https://doi.org/10.1509/jmr.11.0015

13 Mazutis, Daina D., and Slawinski, Natalie. (2015). "Reconnecting business and society: Perceptions of authenticity in corporate social responsibility". *Journal of Business Ethics*, *131*(1), 137–150.
DOI: https://doi.org/10.1007/s10551-014-2253-1

14 Joo, Soyoung., Miller, Elizabeth G., and Fink, Janet S. (2019). "Consumer evaluations of CSR authenticity: Development and validation of a multidimensional CSR authenticity scale". *Journal of Business Research*, *98*, 236–49.
DOI: https://doi.org/10.1016/j.jbusres.2019.01.060

15 Beverland, Michael B., and Farrelly, Francis J. (2010). The quest for authenticity in consumption: Consumers' purposive choice of authentic cues to shape experienced outcomes. *Journal of Consumer Research*, *36*(5), 838–856.

DOI: https://doi.org/10.1086/615047.

16   Dutton, D., 2003. Authenticity in art. *The Oxford handbook of aesthetics*, 258-274.

17   Carroll, Glenn R., (2015). Authenticity: Attribution, value, and meaning. *Emerging trends in the social and behavioral sciences: An interdisciplinary, searchable, and linkable resource*, 1–13.

18   Mirzaei, Abas, Dean C. Wilkie, and Helen Siuki. (2022) "Woke brand activism authenticity or the lack of it." Journal of Business Research 139: 1-12. DOI: https://doi.org/10.1016/j.jbusres.2021.09.044

8

Woke Activism Motivations; Woke Washing Versus Genuine

Many have questioned the motivations of commercial brands getting woke. There is a simple reason for this skepticism. A commercial brand looks for ways to increase sales, or at least survive. Anything they do is for money. If they don't see any financial benefits, they won't get involved.

If brands suddenly become social justice warriors, we assume it's because they smelled money and are fooling progressive teenagers and trying to prevent them from switching to other, unwoke competitors. If a business's DNA is profit, how can you trust them with nonprofit initiatives? I mean, would you adopt a wolf as a pet? It must be a marketing ploy and I won't buy into it, period!

There's no point trying to argue that for-profit businesses aren't primarily concerned with making a profit. But that doesn't necessarily automatically rule out such a business being authentically woke.

When I encounter a woke brand, what I see is a commercial brand with profit-seeking motivations that is searching for the next growth solution. The next strategy is to increase market share, and the next is to extend consumer lifetime value. The next plan is to guarantee long-term survival. That commercial reality has not and will not change, and no one should expect it to change. Any business not concerned with generating revenue and profits won't last long.

Rather than focusing solely on the motives of businesses, we should examine how businesses attempt to achieve their financial goals.

Given there are many apolitical tactics brands can use to generate more revenue, such as investing more in social media advertising or branded content, why do some of them risk alienating much of the public and possibly even much of their target audience?

Why do some brands—brands with the same profit-seeking motivation as their competitors—decide to adopt a polarizing issue that has relevance to the community, as opposed to manipulating consumers with pricing, product updates and distribution? This is a question I'm so interested in.

Can Corporate Self-Interest Improve Societies?

Perhaps we should all be paying more attention to whether there are any benefits for societies when profit-seeking brands become social justice warriors. In other words, given we can't change anything about brands' mercenary motivations, are the citizens of a society better or worse off when some brands shift their focus from traditional marketing methods to more socially responsible communications?

There are two viewpoints to this.

School 1 View: Brands Should Get back to Their Knitting

People may resist and fight back socially responsible communications because they don't trust corporations getting involved in important sociopolitical issues. Especially if an individual mistrusts private businesses to begin with, as many left-of-center people do, they may not be inclined to give those businesses the benefit of the doubt when they claim to have seen the light about pressing social problems.

If I don't trust brands in general, I'll be inclined to view woke brands as wolves in sheep's clothing. That may be the case even when the woke brand is championing a cause I support.

One danger of brands becoming social justice warriors is their lack of experience in addressing, responding to, and effectively communicating woke issues in their marketing campaigns. As we've seen over the past few years, woke brands have often been more successful in alienating, offending, and attacking their target audience than advancing substantial social change. In conventional marketing campaigns (where brands are experienced) there is usually a low degree of sensitivity and tension; the topics addressed in the campaign are often product or service related; and the tone is inspiring and persuasive. It is therefore unlikely that the brand public will take the message personally and feel offended. They may or may not fall in love with the messaging, but they are unlikely to be angered by it.

However, given the nature of woke issues, it is easy for part of the brand public to take the message personally and feel attacked. Applying the typical marketing tools and techniques to sensitive woke topics, it is not surprising to see backlashes and boycotts.

Engaging in (pro-social) issues in conflict with the (pro-profit) nature of the business and applying traditional and typical marketing techniques to untypical issues brands have traditionally avoided are the two reasons people have shown resistance toward wokeness.

School 2 View: Brands Should Do Their Fair Share

People with this view see potential benefits for society if brands engage in important woke issues. The main point of this argument is the fact that, thanks to the consumer dollars they receive, brands are powerful agents that can use their power to have a positive social bearing (or at least try to).

In this line of thinking, discouraging brands from engaging in woke issues can only be good news for brands, given they can simply go back to concentrating on maximizing their profits without needing to worry about making the world a better place.

In a world free of woke brands, brands could get back to all the wrongdoings that School 1 is accusing commercial brands of doing. They can go back to selling products that are made in poor countries, taking advantage of sweatshops filled with child laborers. They can go back to persuasive advertising campaigns that encourage overconsumption, rather than worrying about issues such as treating their workers fairly and not polluting the environment.

This group argues that we support brands with our purchases and that brands need to return the favor and support humanity. School 2 also argues that if I don't fall in love with a brand's woke move, my next option is to fall in love with the additional camera at the back of my smartphone (a functional feature I won't need).

Like it or not, brands are part of our lives. We adopt them, adore them, and praise them. So why not let that engagement be, at least in part, because of a brand's wokeness, with the hope that it may have a positive effect on society?

School 2 argues that a possible gain is better than a sure loss. If brands do engage in woke issues, there is some chance those brands will have a positive social bearing. On the other hand, if brands stay away from woke issues, there is absolutely no chance they will benefit their customers by making the world a better place.

It should be noted that School 2 types aren't naïve. They may be as bemused as their School 1 counterparts at the sight of businesses that have long-evaded paying tax, exploited their employees, engaged with corrupted politicians, and despoiled the environment, reinventing themselves overnight as social justice warriors. But School 2 types are open to believing these businesses have changed their ways, and if not, the public has a reason to hold brands accountable on their woke promises.

Given the widespread and often justified skepticism of corporations' motivations, brands keen to jump on the woke bandwagon will need to provide clear explanations to School 1 and School 2 types about their road-to-Damascus conversion to woke-dom.

Brands that ignore the critiques and just try to tick the woke box will likely encounter woke shaming, protests, and resistance. Brands need to demonstrate the degree to which they are serious about being woke and contributing toward solving sociopolitical issues. They need to provide tangible evidence that their motivations are genuine.

In the following chapters I discuss how brands can remove the pain points in their woke journey and turn them into gain points.

9

Is Low Alignment a Bad Thing?

The degree of alignment between a brand's core business, its image and positioning, and the woke issue can influence perceived woke authenticity. Any misalignment risks backlash and boycotting, whereas a high degree of alignment is likely to increase the perception that the brand is being genuine. To be perceived as authentic, the social responsibility program should be strongly associated with the organization's core values and culture.

To better understand different responses to alignment, consider the following three scenarios.

Scenario 1: Alienated

You have a group of angry consumers who feel betrayed, attacked, and alienated by the brand. Looking for a way to rationalize their anger and justify their criticism, they look at the relevance of the woke issue to the brand's offerings (that is, its products and services).

Scenario 2: Cynical

You have a group of customers or a brand public that is generally cynical toward commercial brands' involvement in prosocial or political moves. While they may not oppose the message the campaign tries to communicate, they question the messenger (that is, the brand).

Scenario 3: Impressed

These are existing or potential customers who are impressed by the woke move and think low fit is a good thing. These customers are likely to make comments, such as, "What a brave move," "Who says there needs to be a prerequisite for woke moves?" and "About time!"

When it comes to the alignment between the brand

positioning, core focus, and the woke move, you are dealing with three different responses.

One challenge that brands face, given they are overseen by humans, is that they suffer from optimism bias. That is, overestimating the likelihood of positive outcomes and underestimating the likelihood of suffering from negative events. Being overexcited about a woke campaign and ignoring the risks of the campaign going wrong can result in an out-of-control negative response that damages the brand.

Optimism bias is one of the reasons brands are shocked and unprepared when their woke campaigns attract criticism rather than garner praise. Treating the woke campaign as a set-and-forget affair, abruptly pulling it when it attracts criticism, or hastily issuing groveling apologies to those claiming to be offended are all signs that those behind a woke campaign have been overly optimistic and haven't prepared for the possibility of negative responses, as well as positive ones.

What if there is a low degree of alignment between the brand focus and the woke topic? Should the brand adopt the "stick to your knitting" approach and stay out of woke activism? Or should the brand ignore the Type 1 (alienated) and Type 2 (cynical) audiences, and just count on those who are in the Type 3 (impressed) audience and who don't seem to be concerned about the lack of alignment or, even better, see the low alignment as a sign of commitment and responsibility? How can a brand still engage in the woke activism, despite the low alignment?

What Is the Motivation to Engage in Low-Alignment Woke Activism?

What is the motivation to engage in a sociopolitical woke activism issue despite a low degree of fit? Most likely the issue is trendy and has gained the attention of the audience because it's linked to a high-profile social movement such as MeToo or Black Lives Matter.

As discussed in previous chapters, the temptation to engage in issues with social currency can be motivated by a desire to benefit from free PR, or in response to the brand public's call out (that is, those who buy the brand expecting it to take a stand). Conforming to the brand public's expectations and becoming a box ticker just to be safe are the main reasons behind engaging in a low-fit woke topic.

However, if the topic is not trendy or linked to a current movement, the low alignment can be interpreted in two different ways: innovation and creativity in woke activism, or change of discussion, distracting the attention of their audience from what is most important to them (which is more related to the focus of their business).

See It as a Brand Extension

Ideally, brands should find relevant and well-aligned woke topics that can resonate with their target audience. If you are a brand manager, source your woke move from an issue that won't negatively surprise or confuse your audience. If your target audience doesn't expect you to engage in a particular issue because they don't see you as having the expertise to intervene, that should be a good indication to avoid that issue.

Woke moves should be seen as a brand extension. However, instead of extending your brand offerings to new categories, you're extending your positioning and brand image. You should address the four key questions of a successful brand extension decision when considering a woke move.

Key questions for successful brand extension

1. Based on what expertise are you extending your brand image to woke activism?
2. Can that expertise be easily transferred?
3. Will the brand public be able to process and understand the connection between your expertise and the woke issue?
4. Will the brand public find you a credible agent to champion woke activism?

As a brand that moves into woke activism territory, you want to know the ingredient, expertise, or specialty you're bringing to the new area and which the target audience may benefit from. To take a hypothetical non-woke example, imagine Kentucky Fried Chicken (KFC) announces they will launch KFC airlines. How would the target audience react to this? Just because I love KFC's popcorn chicken doesn't mean I'll book my next flight with KFC Airlines. Similarly, Intel Inside extending into selling ice cream may not be necessarily a successful extension because consumers evaluate the extension based on the questions listed above. On the other hand, the brand public familiar with Virgin knows its brand has no boundaries and can be expected to extend to any industry. Virgin Airlines, Virgin Money, and Virgin Mobile are a few examples.

When it comes to woke activism, it is the same evaluation process. If there aren't good answers to the four key questions, then the target audience may struggle to find the connection and, as a result, fail to support the brand's woke move.

Prior to 2019, people thought of Gillette as a company that had a core focus of providing shaving products. And prior to 2019, Gillette's communicated messages were exclusively, or at least mainly, about the superiority of its shaving products and the role those products could play in helping men achieve social, sexual, and career success.

Then, in the wake of the MeToo movement, Gillette ran its "The best a man can be" campaign, encouraging men to call out other men for toxic masculine behavior. Both supporters and critics of the campaign had to account for the sudden change in Gillette's communicated message. Critics zeroed in on the supposed mismatch between Gillette's core purpose (helping men groom themselves) and its sudden enthusiasm for a feminist cause.

This resulted in social media comments, such as

"Say goodbye to my business. Stick to advertising razors in the future."

"Gillette, can you get back to advertising shavers?"

"Stick to making razors and commercials about razors."

"Why is a razor company making commercials about the minority of males who are toxic rather than about shaving? Shouldn't you focus on advertising your products?"

"Why don't you just stick to making razors and shaving cream, losers."

10

The Danger of Cute Woke Moves

Walking the Talk

We all have heard the phrase "walk the talk." Another important factor when judging the authenticity of a brand is the extent to which the brand is living up to, and is committed to delivering, what it promises.[1] Practice is an essential factor in evaluating the authenticity of the brand's woke activist move.

Many brands rushing into wokeness and purposefulness forget that they aren't just what you communicate in your brand messages. It is what you practice internally. In fact, whatever a brand promises will be added to the "How to evaluate this brand" list.

Every time a brand becomes a social justice warrior, every time it lectures society about how to be more meaningful and purposeful, every time it seeks attention by making a "look how woke I am" move, it is creating new expectations that it will need to live up to. Every time a brand makes a claim, the brand public is quick to judge the degree of truth in that claim by looking for tangible cues. If those tangible cues are not easily found, or if there is no substantial proof point, then the brand public not only question the authenticity, they call out the brand for false claims. Woke moves are a double-edged sword; they can work brilliantly but can also result in the brand public digging deep into a business's internal practices, then criticizing those practices.

Practice is the element that marries intangible virtuousness with tangible proof points. One reason brands are called social justice warriors in a mocking way is because they have decided overnight to advocate for wokeness without offering evidence that what they advocate is greatly in sync with what they do. A brand's failure to practice what it preaches means its woke move will likely be perceived as a theatrical, opportunistic show of lecturing society, which will inevitably result in accusations of woke washing.

Cute Woke Moves

Turning the M in your brand logo upside down so it resembles a W to celebrate International Women's Day is a cute, attention-grabbing move. But it is just empty symbolism unless the brand can outline how it practices celebrating and empowering women during the other 364 days of the year.

Posting a black square on Instagram during Blackout Tuesday is a cute move. But it lacks substance and is merely symbolic. For instance, after launching its Race Together campaign,[2] Starbucks soon realized that their move was perhaps too cute and learned the hard way how important it is to back up your cute woke moves. While being a woke advocate can be effective in fighting injustice, advocating without practicing will backfire and can result in brand hijack and boycott.

This can be explained by expectancy theory, or more precisely, expectancy theory violation. A brand makes a promise, creates an expectation, and then it doesn't deliver at all, or underdelivers. Recently, M&M's launched rebranded much-loved characters, adding cute wokeness, thereby symbolically repositioning the brand as inclusive. As reported by CNN, Mars's president, Anton Vincent, labelled it a subtle cue, offering a more representative female character. However, people had mixed feelings. Some mocked the move and questioned whether people were still allowed to eat the characters.

Symbolic moves to offer a sense of belonging and community that have no substance and therefore minimal effect cannot and should not be labelled woke, unless backed by additional supportive impactful measures that have real long-term influence on people's lives. Otherwise, it may risk being mocked by the public and the media, which is a method of resistance to status quo.

Humor, ridicule, and mockery are solutions that the public and media use to defend the status quo (and, interestingly, to challenge it). Now, if you factor out political ideologies and

Alternatively – this is why conservatives use the term "woke" mockingly and define wokeness as usually rooted in social (capital & not sincerity)

71

conservative values and still see a great degree of brand ridicule, even from those with progressive values, it should be a good sign the move hasn't been so effective in challenging the status quo. In this case even the *Washington Post* published an opinion piece ridiculing the M&M's rebrand move.[3]

Brands trying to be woke by reaching for low-hanging fruit, and making light or cute woke moves, turn themselves into easy targets for those trying to maintain the status quo. The outcome can be woke shaming, which is not exactly what those affected by discrimination want. Trying to make your brand more relevant by only touching the surface and not digging deep to find impactful solutions for sociopolitical issues can hurt the woke movement.

Over the last decade, many corporations have made cute moves to signal their support for Black Lives Matter, only to then be taken to task about their failure to either hire black people or promote them to senior positions. To use the academic terminology, they created an expectancy theory violation. They rushed to make a cute move, only to find it resulted in scrutiny and criticism rather than free publicity and applause.

Failure to deliver what has been promised and the inconsistency between the communicated message and the brand's previous practices can result in a perception of woke washing. Woke activism campaigns that can demonstrate that a brand practices what it preaches are more likely to be seen as authentic. That's because they can show that they can go beyond advocacy and make commitments toward tangible and intangible practices, aligning the practice with the company's values and purpose.

The Missing Element of Uber's Successful Ad Campaign

Uber ran the "Tonight, I'll Be Eating ..." ad series. It featured a range of local and international celebrities who were all trying different foods via Uber Eats. While it was a clever communication and promotion strategy, it missed the mark on Uber's promise of employee inclusion, which was to empower its network of drivers.

In more than fifty different episodes of this ad series, you never see a driver in the picture, only a hand delivering the food. In a separate campaign, which we will discuss in more detail later in this book, Uber delivers a clear message that if you tolerate racism, you should delete Uber.

A brand committed to playing a role in sociopolitical issues has somehow forgotten to practice the mindset it preaches in its otherwise engaging campaign. While running ads showing food being delivered to celebrities, Uber could have also empowered and championed its (often overlooked) drivers. Uber could also have gone beyond featuring celebrities and shown drivers delivering food to those affected by racism or domestic violence survivors, or other ordinary Uber Eats customers. That would have provided a more congruent picture of the brand's inclusive values.

References

1 Napoli, Julie., Dickinson, Sonia J., Beverland, Michael B., and Farrelly, Francis. (2014). "Measuring consumer-based brand authenticity". *Journal of Business Research*, 67(6), 1090–1098. DOI: https://doi.org/10.1016/j.jbusres.2013.06.001

2 Peterson, Hayley. "The real story behind Starbucks' most embarrassing moment in history", *Business Insider,* June 15, 2015.

https://www.businessinsider.com/starbucks-race-together-campaign-history-2015-6.

3   Petri, Alexandra. 9 questions I have about the new, more 'inclusive' M&M mascots, *Washington Post,* January 20, 2022. https://www.washingtonpost.com/opinions/2022/01/20/mm-mascots-inclusive-rebrand-satire/.

11

History and Expectations

A brand's woke history can be defined as the brand public's knowledge and perception of the brand's track record of engaging in pro-social or political initiatives. If the brand has a history of engaging in activism and controversial higher-purpose moves, and if the brand is known for championing social and political issues, corporate sociopolitical activism is likely to be perceived more positively by the brand public. Based on attribution theory,[1] the knowledge consumers have about a brand can help them to assess the degree to which the move is self-serving or public-serving.[2] An individual's knowledge about the company is vital because consumers need to rely on the company's history to determine whether it has a genuine interest in a cause.

Companies with strong histories of being socially responsible are consistently seen as public-serving.[2] The knowledge of a brand's previous social responsibility practices can also help the brand public to evaluate why a company is conducting such acts.[2]

Brands that don't have any history of practicing purposefulness and pro-social moves and abruptly get involved in wokeness may confuse the brand public, which is likely to wonder why the brand is taking such stands and representing itself as a social justice warrior. Thus, having a preexisting relevant history and positioning can facilitate the brand public's understanding and decoding of woke moves.

For instance, Ben & Jerry's has a history of getting involved in hot-button issues. So even if they don't always agree with its activist campaigns, people who buy their products understand taking controversial political stances is to be expected from the brand.

Social media comments, such as the following, reflect that understanding.

"I will always support this company because of their awareness of real-life problems."

"Much respect. What excellent role models you are for doing the right thing, time and time again."

"This isn't the first time you guys took a dumb-a*s stance on something you know nothing about, so I'm not surprised."

Expectation Theory

History is also linked to the individual's expectations of the brand. One key source of information for the brand public, according to expectancy theory, is the past actions of a brand.[4] It can influence how the brand public may evaluate the brand's future social initiatives.[5, 4] Building on the expectancy violations perspective,[6, 7] brands with a history of engaging in pro-social moves may be expected to be more responsible and accountable, compared to firms with low pro-social performance.[4] If influenced by their preexisting perceptions and knowledge, consumers expect a brand to engage in social and political advocacy, which may influence the outcome and how they respond to wokeness.

One mistake brands make when engaging in woke activism is that they use the social issue to build brand image, or to reposition their brand (usually after a few rough years of having a bad reputation resulting from unethical or irresponsible business practices).

Just as a good history of social responsibility and accountability can have a positive effect on the perception of the brand public, a bad history of social irresponsibility has a profound negative impact—an impact much stronger than the positive effect of the brand public responding enthusiastically to a woke move.

Negativity Bias

According to negativity bias theory (that is, people's tendency to register negative stimuli and to retrieve them more often), people value negative information more than positive information. Psychologist John Gottman famously demonstrated the power of negative feelings and memories over positive ones. The "Gottman magic ratio of 5 to 1" asserts that one bad experience is as impactful as five good ones (i.e., for each bad experience and associated negative feelings you will need to create five good experiences). In the context of woke activism, that means a brand with a previous bad reputation and social irresponsibility is more likely to trigger a strong negative consumer response, at least initially, when it starts making woke moves.

Previous Irresponsibility and Scandal

Previous research identifies three types of consumer response to social irresponsibility:

- automatic response;
- automatic appraisal response; and
- social cognitive response.

Automatic response manifests in forms of anger and disgust, and those feelings can be seen as informational to the person experiencing them, as well as to those observing them.[8]

Automatic appraisal response: As well an automatic emotional response, the brand public may show an automatic appraisal response, evaluating the brand's perceived social irresponsibility from good to bad, or from favorable to unfavourable.[9] Automatic evaluation also involves an appraisal of the degree of social irresponsibility significance. Both automatic emotional and evaluative responses can mediate the effect such irresponsibility may have on consumers' behavioral responses.[8]

Social cognitive response: This is the third type of reaction to social irresponsibility. Previous experiences influence and form social cognitions in social process and psychological developments.[8] Automatic emotional and evaluative responses to social irresponsibility can be influenced by social cognition. Previous experiences and awareness of social irresponsibility can influence emotional, evaluative, and social cognition of the public[8] and ultimately how the brand public reacts to a firm's future pro-social moves.

Related to a brand's history, any previous scandals or acts of social irresponsibility that are fresh in consumers' memories are likely to resurface when a brand pulls a woke move, and this can have an effect on how the brand public perceives the sacrifice (for instance, risking losing customers and revenue) involved in that move.

While a lack of preexisting positioning may not have a positive effect on the perception, previous irresponsible acts and scandals are likely to have a negative effect on the outcomes of brand sacrifice.

For instance, Uber has frequently been accused of treating its drivers poorly. So when Uber made a woke move (encouraging people to delete the Uber app if they tolerate racism), many urged the business to get its own house in order before daring to try to eliminate racism in the United States.

Likewise, whenever Nike makes a woke move, there are members of the brand public who waste no time in reminding people that Nike has long outsourced production to sweatshops in developing countries, such as Bangladesh.

To summarize, having a history of social accountability and responsibility can have a positive influence on the perceived woke authenticity. But previous social irresponsibility can have a much greater effect on the perception of woke inauthenticity.

References

1   Kelley, Harold H. (1967). Attribution theory in social psychology. In D. Levine (ed.), *Nebraska Symposium on Motivation*, 15, 192– 240. Lincoln, NE: University of Nebraska Press.

2   Alhouti, Sarah., Johnson, Catherine. M., and Holloway, Betsy B. (2016). "Corporate social responsibility authenticity: Investigating its antecedents and outcomes". *Journal of Business Research*, *69*(3), 1242–1249.
    DOI: https://doi.org/10.1016/j.jbusres.2015.09.007

3   Nardella, Giuliu., Brammer, Stephen. and Surdu, Irina. (2020). "Shame on who? The effects of corporate irresponsibility and social performance on organizational reputation". *British Journal of Management*, *31*(1), 5-23.
    DOI: https://doi.org/10.1111/1467-8551.12365

4   Wei, Jiuchang., Ouyang, Zhe., and Chen, Haipeng. (2017). "Well known or well liked? The effects of corporate reputation on firm value at the onset of a corporate crisis." *Strategic Management Journal*, 38, 2103– 2120.
    DOI: https://doi-org.simsrad.net.ocs.mq.edu.au/10.1002/smj.2639

5   Bailey, Ainsworth A., and Bonifield, Caroline M. (2010). "Broken (promotional) promises: The impact of firm reputation and blame." *Journal of Marketing Communications*, *16*(5), 287–306.
    DOI: https://doi-org.simsrad.net.ocs.mq.edu.au/10.1080/13527260902920690

6   Burgoon, Judee K. (1978). "A communication model of personal space violations: explication and an initial test", *Human Communication Research*, *4*, 129– 42.
    DOI: 10.1111/j.1468-2958.1978.tb00603.x

7   Xie, Chunyan., and Bagozzi, Richard P. (2019). "Consumer responses to corporate social irresponsibility: The role of moral emotions, evaluations, and social cognitions." *Psychology & Marketing*, *36*(6), 565–86.
    DOI: https://doi-org.simsrad.net.ocs.mq.edu.au/10.1002/mar.21197

8   Judge, Timothy.A. and Kammeyer-Mueller, John D., 2012. "Job attitudes". *Annual review of psychology*, *63*, 341–67.
    https://doi.org/10.1146/annurev-psych-120710-100511

12

Inclusion and Diversity

Perhaps one of the most frequently created new corporate roles in recent years has been head of diversity and inclusion. Companies have been creating new roles, organizing staff training sessions, and inviting guest speakers to better align their internal practices with fast-changing social norms. After the death of George Floyd in mid2020 by a former convicted police officer who knelt on Floyd's neck for more than nine minutes, many brands were accused on different social media platforms of misrepresenting their hiring and promotion practices in their branding and advertising communications, in relation to African Americans and ethnic minorities in general.

In response, brands started reviewing their internal practices and embracing inclusion and diversity. Brands that had expressed solidarity with the African American community came under scrutiny from their brand publics and were frequently criticized for being opportunistic and hypocritical.

Brands that thought it was safe to post a black square on their Instagram page during the Blackout Tuesday were suddenly in the spotlight and had nowhere to hide. They now needed to explain how their ad campaigns only featured certain skin tones, ethnicities, body shapes, ages, and genders. Brands had to act quickly to stay out of controversy and minimize brand damage. So they started making promises and outlining how they were going to make it up to those misrepresented communities and hadn't served well in the past.

They posted "We heard you and we will do better" proclamations on social media. For instance, after making a woke move in relation to Black Lives Matter that attracted criticism, Adidas released a follow-up post (after initially just expressing solidarity) outlining the steps they would take to support the Black and Latino communities. (One initiative was the introduction of a new quota requiring that 30 percent of all future hires be Black or Latino.)

Likewise, Netflix removed controversial movies, such as *Gone with the Wind*, while the TV show *The Bachelor* announced its first Black bachelor for the upcoming season.

This was the point where brands thought the best and fastest approach to inclusion and diversity was to practice R&R: removing and replacing. That is

- removing their discriminatory practices and erasing their history of exclusion and unequal opportunities; and
- replacing white with Black men with women, straight with LGBTIQA+, and so forth.

How Do We Define Social Inclusion?

Licsandru and Chi Cui (2018), reviewing the existing literature on social inclusion, define social inclusion as "the individual's feelings of belongingness to a host society in which he or she feels accepted, empowered, respected, and fully recognized as an equal member" (330).

Source: Licsandru and Chi Cui (2018)

They propose five key aspects of social inclusion:

- acceptance;
- belongingness;
- empowerment;
- equality; and
- respect.

Acceptance is defined as, "One's feeling that other people wish to include him/her in the host society," which highlights the need for recognition and a feeling of being welcomed and accepted.

Belongingness, which is closely related to the acceptance dimension, is defined as "One's cognitive judgment of fit and emotional connectedness to the host society."

If the perception of acceptance is achieved, it is likely that the individual feels they are connected to society and belong to a community that has accepted them.

The feeling of acceptance and belongingness may lead to

the perception of relative powerfulness. This is defined as "One's feeling of control, contribution to and self-efficacy within the host society, being involved in decision making processes." An individual who feels powerful tends to actively make decisions to make their lives better, and to play an active role in fighting stigma and powerlessness.

Equality and respect are the final two dimensions of social inclusion. They are also the most relevant aspects of inclusion in the context of socio-political justice and wokeness. Equality—that is, an indicator of social inclusion in public policy [2]—involves concepts such as fairness, justice, and balance.[3]

An individual may feel equal by being equal before the law or having equal opportunities.[4, 5] Respect is defined as "something to which we should presume every human being has a claim, namely for full recognition as a person, with the same basic moral worth as any other."[6]

Upsetting versus Disappointing

One straightforward approach to inclusion is neutrality. Especially in the political context, being inclusive simply meant staying neutral and not taking a side.

However, staying neutral is no longer an option, and if it doesn't upset one group, it may disappoint another. A brand that is perceived to not be part of the solution (to racism, sexism, homophobia, or transphobia) is likely to be accused of being part of the problem.

In 1998, when the African American community expected Michael Jordan, one of America's most influential African American sports figures, to support Democrat senate candidate Harvey Gantt, who was running against Jesse Helms (a racist Republican), Michael Jordan refused to do so, saying, "Republicans buy sneakers too."

Neutrality's Problematic Nature

As documented in the documentary *The Last Dance*, that disappointed many people. Jordan's refusal to endorse someone poised to become the first African American to represent North Carolina in the Senate was perceived by some as evidence Jordan was prioritizing profit over principles.

Of course, had Jordan supported the Democrat candidate he would have upset many of his Republican fans. On the other hand, not taking a stand and remaining neutral resulted in him disappointing lots of his African American fans.

So it is always a dance on the edge of upsetting versus disappointing. In the past, it was common for prominent athletes and other celebrities to keep their political views to themselves. However, it is no longer so easy to try to remain popular by not upsetting anyone.

That noted, in less partisan, mostly social and nonpolitical context, neutrality can be perceived as a practice of inclusion without undergoing removing and replacing. Those feeling upset and alienated by corporations' inclusion and diversity moves want brands to adopt a language that doesn't attack or question them because of their immutable characteristics or ideologies.

On the other hand, those who believe they are not supported and empowered by the wider society often expect influential public figures and powerful brands to empower underrepresented communities, ethnicities, genders, races, and age groups.

African American journalist Nathan McCall summarized these expectations in 1989 (almost twenty years before Nike's Dream Crazy narrative) when he said, "You should stand for something, even if it means sacrificing a payday."

References

1 Licsandru, Tana C. and Cui, Charles C. (2018). "Subjective Social Inclusion: A Conceptual Critique For Socially Inclusive Marketing". Journal Of Business Research, 82, 330–39.

DOI: https://doi.org/10.1016/j.jbusres.2017.08.036

2   Collins, Hugh. (2003). "Discrimination, Equality, and Social Inclusion." *The Modern Law Review*, 66 (1), 16–43.
    DOI: https://doi.org/10.1111/1468-2230.6601002

3   Lunga, Violet. (2002). "Empowerment through inclusion: The case of women in the discourses of advertising in Botswana." *Perspectives on Global Development and Technology*, 1(1), 35–50.

4   Davys, Deborah., and Tickle, Ellen (2008). "Social inclusion and valued roles: A supportive framework". *International Journal of Therapy and Rehabilitation*, 15(8), 2–7.
    DOI: 10.12968/ijtr.2008.15.8.30820

5   Zelenev, Sergei. (2009). "Social integration in a contemporary world". *Global Social Policy*, 9(1), 6–9.
    DOI: https://doi.org/10.1177/1468018109009001080 2

6   Hill, T. E. Jr. *Respect, Pluralism, and Justice*. Oxford University Press, 2000.

13

Woke Sacrifice

According to costly signaling theory, brands committed to fighting discrimination and becoming woke activists need to signal the extent to which they're prepared to show costly responsibility and sacrifice profit and revenue in their support of socially and politically charged movements such as BLM and MeToo.

Costly signaling suggests a brand's woke move is more likely to be perceived as credible and authentic if it involves financial and nonfinancial sacrifices for the brand. I call this *brand sacrifice* and define it as the extent to which a brand is giving up on potential profits and risking future revenue to support its brand advocacy moves.

I argue that brands employing brand activism move as a mechanism to stay relevant to their target audience and show not just responsibility but also accountability need to make costly signals. That is, they need to put their money where their mouth is and sacrifice revenue and profit for the greater good. Patagonia's Please Don't Buy Our Jacket campaign, seeking to discourage environmentally damaging overconsumption, is an example of brand sacrifice because it encourages consumers to think twice before purchasing Patagonia's products.

While this may contradict the general perception that brands' ultimate risk and nightmare is consumer boycott, we're observing the migration of brands into territories that on paper seem suicidal, brand discouraging consumers from buying their offerings. Campaigns, such as the ones Uber has run, encouraging consumers to look elsewhere if their values aren't in sync with the values a brand is standing on is one example.

In the past it has always been the other way around, and brands have been threatened with boycotts by consumers due to the lack of self-brand connection and out of sync consumer-brand values. Now it appears that brands are threatening to boycott consumers and decide who is worthy of their products and services.

But this is precisely what I define as brand sacrifice: the degree

Examples of Brand Sacrifice

to which a brand is prepared to risk revenue when taking a stance on higher-purpose values.

Brand sacrifice can also involve making a costly change in response to the brand public's call outs. Renaming a brand due to its supposed racist connotations (Aunt Jemima products are now Pearl Milling ones, just as Uncle Ben's products are now Ben's Original), or pulling a product due to its perceived links to slavery (such as Nike's Betsy Ross flag shoe line) are examples of costly signaling precisely because they involved a lot of expense and effort.

Costly signaling involves risking the ultimate objective of a commercial brand—generating revenue and profit. In contrast, costless signaling involves superficial virtue signaling and just being one of the many brands that attempt to tick the box of social responsibility,

Costly signaling allows brands to stay relevant and appeal to the target audience, but it requires concrete moves that show the brand is prepared to take a financial hit to fight against social injustices.

In addition to the examples provided earlier in this chapter, there are other recent cases of brand sacrifice moves. For instance, the Uber billboard ad, which was also posted on their social media pages, proclaims, "If you tolerate racism, delete Uber." There's also Ben & Jerry's announcement that it would stop selling ice cream in the Occupied Palestinian Territory. These moves, as compared to just posting a black square on Instagram, or posting a statement of support on Twitter, may potentially negatively affect the brand's future revenue and profit.

Factors Contributing to the Success or Failure of Brand Sacrifice

The main motivation of brands engaged in brand sacrifice is to become or to stay relevant to their desired target audience. But from a business's point of view, the question is how to minimize the risk of negatively affecting the future revenue.

Understanding the factors that may influence the success or failure of brand sacrifice can help brand managers to make brand sacrifice moves that minimize the possibility of a backlash and maximize the target audience's support. There are several factors that may contribute to brand sacrifice success or failure. I've labelled them the TRIC principles.

TRIC Principles

The TRIC principles are trendiness, risk, irresponsibility, and choice and are explained in further detail as follows.

Trendiness

The extent to which the brand sacrifice is linked to topical social and political issues is defined as brand sacrifice trendiness. Brand sacrifice issues tend to be trendy and a response to high-profile social and political tensions in society.

Brands choosing trendy sociopolitical issues are motivated to be perceived as legitimate by their audience. The trendiness of brand sacrifice moves can be perceived by the public as an attempt to passively conform to the call out, or it can be perceived as a proactive strategy.

The trendiness of brand sacrifice moves can therefore influence the perception of the brand public. Brand sacrifice moves that are less trendy and more independent of the social and political context are more likely to be perceived more positively, all else being equal. But if a brand chooses trendy sociopolitical issues, there is a chance it will be accused of being opportunistic and pursuing financial benefits, which will trigger negative emotions in the brand public. Trendiness can contribute toward the perception of a brand that they care for the society.

Risk

Does the target audience appreciate the risks a brand takes to become a woke activist? The extent to which the brand public perceives the brand sacrifice move as a clear risk to the business's survival is defined as "the perceived risk of brand sacrifice." Reputational and financial risk are two types of risks that the brand public may evaluate when considering the brand sacrifice move.

Reputational risk arises from the partisan nature of brand sacrifice moves. While the brand is using the sacrifice to appeal to a certain section of the brand public, there is a risk of alienating another section of it.

Similarly, a brand's sacrifice move can be seen as sabotaging its future revenue. After all, those offended by the sacrifice move may try to avoid the brand and switch to competitors. If the brand public can see the reputational and financial risks a brand is taking, there is a greater likelihood the target audience will accept and support the sacrifice move. However, if the brand public perceives the risk as minor and calculated, with a manageable effect on the brand, it may not be so accepted and supported

Refusing to sell a product to a certain group of consumers in a certain region because of a conflict of values is seen as a high-stakes move. For instance, many found Ben & Jerry's withdrawal from the Occupied Palestinian Territory enormously risky. But this move allowed Ben & Jerry to signal the degree to which they were serious and determined to express their support for Palestine.

Irresponsibility

When brands become social justice warriors and attempt bold moves that put their revenue and survival at risk, their previous wrongdoings and practice failures suddenly come into play. A lack of previous activism is something the brand public may tolerate. But corporate irresponsibility and wrong practices aren't easy to forget.

In other words, while a lack of preexisting positioning may not have a positive effect on the brand public perception, previous scandals are likely to have a negative result. Any previous controversies that are still fresh in consumers' memories are likely to resurface and effect on how the brand public perceives the sacrifice.

For example, Uber has been associated with ill treatment of its drivers, in particular charging them an exorbitant service fee. When Uber "went woke," its poor treatment of its contractors was referenced in relation to its brand sacrifice move and many urged the brand to reform its own practices before trying to reform the wider society.

Choice

Consumers may respond differently to brand sacrifice, depending on the choice of brand sacrifice. There are different types of brand sacrifice (i.e., the discontinuation of a product offering, a rebrand, or product purchase discouragement) and the brand public responds differently depending on the sacrifice in question.

For example, Uncle Ben's rebrand got a mixed response. The brand public wasn't too sure if the brand rename was the best way to show a commitment to reducing racism. Dropping the word Uncle and removing the Black farmer (which was the visual character of the brand) was perceived by many as a move toward racism, and against diversity and inclusion. It seems that most of the brand public expected Uncle Ben's to keep and celebrate the Black farmer character.

Likewise, Ben & Jerry's decision to stop selling ice cream in the Occupied Palestinian Territory also confused and divided its brand public. Many people questioned how such a decision would help resolve the conflict between Israel and Palestine.

So even when the brand sacrifice is perceived as risky, brands may not benefit if the brand public perceives the risky move as misguided or meaningless.

14

Social Currency

Over time, different issues attract the interest of the public. When different movements attract media attention, brands often come under pressure from their target audience to take a stand and express their support for, say, anti-racism or female empowerment.

This is because brands are seen as social-change facilitators capable of addressing societal and cultural tensions in a way that allows those brands to build relevance, stay in sync with progressive values, and become iconic.[1, 2] And when brands show responsibility in tackling social issues and tensions, they can seize opportunities to build a higher purpose.[3] In tackling social issues, some brands take a patient approach while others adopt an impatient approach that is built on current and trendy social issues.

Brands like Chobani remain steadfastly committed to a higher purpose (i.e., better food for more people and investing in social entrepreneurship),[4] regardless of which hashtags are trending on social media. Brands such as Chobani take a slow-cooked, patient approach to fixing social issues.

In contrast, woke campaigns are based on topical issues and attempt to affect rapid and dramatic social change.

Bandwagoning and its effect on consumer perceptions can be explained by neo-institutional theory. Brands choosing trendy sociopolitical issues are motivated to be perceived as legitimate by their audience. Legitimacy is defined by Meyer and Scott (1983) as "the degree of cultural support for an organization."[5] Firms seeking legitimacy aim to offer acceptable corporate behavior that addresses questions posed by institutional actors.[6, 7]

Companies often engage in legitimacy-seeking behavior to secure the organization's future survival.[8] Companies may adopt two key legitimacy-seeking strategies: passively conforming to external pressures,[9, 10, 11] or proactively adopting strategies to manage external pressures.[12, 13]

Bandwagon Bias Heuristic Theory

Mimetic, normative, and coercive isomorphism are three types of passive conformation strategies proposed by Di Maggio and Powell (1983). In particular, mimetic conformation is the direct response to uncertainty. In the context of woke activism, it leads companies to mimic referenced behaviors of other organizations. [14]

Such a response can also be explained by the bandwagon bias heuristic theory, which is defined as thinking an attitude or object—such as an idea, issue, or a story—is good because others, such as peers or other organizations [15] think it is.

The trendiness of woke moves can be perceived by the public as an attempt to passively conform to the callout, or it can be perceived as a proactive strategy that is a cultural currency, [16] facilitating the capture of intermediate non-economic and economic inputs from external constituents. The trendiness of woke moves can therefore influence the perception of the brand public in relation to the motivations of brands.

Social media comments, like the ones below, show bandwagoning perception of trendy woke moves.

"Just following the trends so people like them more and buy more of them."

"Companies have rebranded before and then disappeared altogether. Jumping on a bandwagon doesn't solve anything. As a company, you could look to better, more useful ways of making an impact."

Choosing a trendy sociopolitical issue associated with movements such as TimesUp, MeToo, and BLM has a great risk of being perceived as opportunistic.

Bandwagoning versus Brave

When it was announced that the next Superman will be bisexual, some called it bandwagoning and some called it brave. Reported by the BBC, Dean Cain, who stared in *Lois & Clark: The New Adventures of Superman* from 1993 to 1997, labelled the move bandwagoning, arguing that it would have been perceived as brave twenty years ago. This can again be another act of mimetic confirmation, making a symbolic move to signal inclusion with a mixed response from the brand public due to its social currency element.

References

1   Holt, Douglas B. *How brands become icons: The principles of cultural branding.* Harvard Business Publishing. 2004.
2   Pineda, Antonio, Paloma Sanz-Marcos, and María-Teresa Gordillo-Rodríguez. (2020). "Branding, culture, and political ideology: Spanish patriotism as the identity myth of an iconic brand." *Journal of Consumer Culture*, 22 (1): 1–12.
3   Vilá, Omar R., and Sundar Bharadwaj. (2017). Competing on social purpose: Brands that win by tying mission to growth. *Harvard Business Review*, *95*: 94–101.
4   Mainwaring, Simon. *Purpose At Work: How Chobani Builds A Purposeful Culture Around Social Impact. Forbes*, August 27 2018. https://www.forbes.com/sites/simonmainwaring/2018/08/27/how-chobani-builds-a-purposeful-culture-around-social-impact/#24ec51a020f7.
5   Meyer, John W. (1983). "Centralization and the legitimacy problems of local government." *Organizational Environments: Ritual and Rationality,* 199–215.
6   Hamann, Ralph, and Nicola Acutt. (2010). "How should civil society (and the government) respond to 'corporate social responsibility'? A critique of business motivations and the potential for partnerships." *Development Southern Africa*, *20*(2): 255–270.
7   Beddewela, Eshani, and Jenny Fairbrass. (2016). "Seeking legitimacy through CSR: Institutional pressures and corporate responses

of multinationals in Sri Lanka." *Journal of Business Ethics*, *136*(3): 503–522.

8   Sonpar, Karan, Federica Pazzaglia, and Jurgita Kornijenko. (2009). "The Paradox and constraints of legitimacy." *Journal of Business Ethics*, *95*(1): 1–21.

9   DiMaggio, Paul J., and Walter W. Powell. (1983). "The iron cage revisited: Institutional isomorphism and collective rationality in organizational fields." *American Sociological Review*, *48*: 147–160.

10   Meyer, John. W., and Rowan, Brian. (1977). "Institutionalized organizations: formal structure as myth and ceremony." *American Journal of Sociology*, 83 (2): 340–363.

11   Powell, Walter W., and DiMaggio., Paul J. (Eds.). (1991). *The new institutionalism in organizational analysis*. Chicago: The University of Chicago Press.

12   Pfeffer, Jeffrey. (1978). *Organizational design. Arlignton Heights*, IL: A. H. M. Publishing.

13   Oliver, Christine. (1991). "Strategic responses to institutional processes." *The Academy of Management Review*, 16(1): 145–179.

14   Martínez Ferrero, Jennifer., and García-Sánchez, Isabel-María. (2017). "Coercive, normative and mimetic isomorphism as determinants of the voluntary assurance of sustainability reports." *International Business Review*, *26*(1): 102–118.

15   Sundar, S. Shyam., Xu, Qian., and Oeldorf-Hirsch, Anne. (2009). Authority vs. peer: How interface cues influence users. In CHI'09 Extended Abstracts on human factors in computing systems, 4231–4236.

16   Ashforth, Blake E., and Gibbs, Barrie W. (1990). The double-edge of organizational legitimation. *Organization science*, 1(2), 177–194.

15

Resisting versus Questioning the Status Quo in Sociopolitical Conflicts

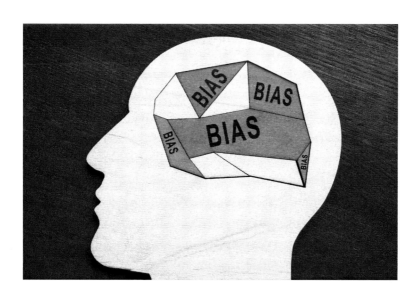

Why do people resist the status quo? And how do they perceive and react to those questioning the status quo?

Those resisting the status quo have mostly been labelled and stereotyped as conservatives, resisting progressive values. However, the motivation to maintain the status quo does not necessarily mean that someone is conservative. One motivation to maintain the status quo is the risk of a power shift. In fact, it is the perceived power that works as the engine for maintaining the status quo. If I feel powerful, changing the status quo may put my perceived power at risk.

I can feel powerful as a political leader, a singer, or a celebrity influencer. Powerful individuals tend to want to maintain the status quo and tend to stereotype their opponents (those questioning the status quo) as extreme activists.

Research shows that powerful individuals who benefit from the status quo are more likely to demonstrate judgmental bias and label less powerful individuals seeking change as extremists.

Defending or changing the status quo can be associated with two types of effects—the target effect and the observer effect. Previous research, mostly undertaken by Professor Dacher Keltner, shows how the different camps perceive and evaluate the power dynamics. Based on the target effect, those pushing to change the status quo are likely to be judged more negatively compared to those trying to maintain the status quo. However, based on the observer effect, those advancing the status quo tend to react more strongly and offer less accurate judgments.

The Noise Effect in Judgment

As Daniel Kahneman (author of *Thinking Fast and Slow*) mentions in his recent book, *Noise*, that whenever there is a judgment, there is noise[1].

Human judgment is subject to background noise. Whenever

we evaluate a cue that we're exposed to, we subconsciously rely on our knowledge about the message and the sender. The part of the equation we tend to unintentionally overlook is ourselves—the receivers of the message. Our judgment is driven by the noises surrounding us. In reality, even the best judges are sometimes terribly inaccurate, being easily outperformed by a machine-learning algorithm that can provide better prediction and evaluations.

Imagine going to a shooting arcade. You have one rifle and five bullets. According to Kahneman and his colleagues, Team A represents an ideal scenario where all shots will be on target, in the bull's eye. Team B represents a biased category, where shots are off target, but concentrated in one area, away from the bull's eye. You may fall into Team C, which is called noisy. Your shots are off target but there is no clear pattern, and the shots are scattered randomly around the bull's eye. If you're not in any of those teams, then you must be Team D, a mix of noisy and biased, where your shots are scattered but not entirely random (e.g., they are systematically, for instance scattered but mostly on one side of the target).

People were destroying their Nike shoes and socks to protest Nike's Colin Kaepernick ad campaign.[2]

In our judgments, we may make random mistakes, or we may make systematic mistakes, or a mix of both. While in a shooting arcade, noises might be controlled. But in our real, day-to-day judgments, controlling for the noise in judgment is not easy. Thus, our judgments and responses to what we're exposed to involve noise and inaccuracy.

Are you a type of person who makes random mistakes or systematic errors?

In the context of woke brand activism, a range of different noises influence how we perceive the stimuli and the risks involved in each brand cue or message. Below, I classify them into macro and micro noises.

Sociopolitical and Environmental Ideologies Contribute to the Noise in Judgment

On August 14, 2016, when Colin Kaepernick started protesting police brutality and social injustice by sitting and not standing during the national anthem, a major noise in judgment started flaming political ideology and patriotic beliefs, thanks to his method of protest. Even though he changed his method of protest from sitting to kneeling (like when soldiers show respect to a fallen solder), because he was criticized by at the time US president Donald Trump, Kaepernick's fight against social injustice became a politically charged move. You can imagine the noise in judgment experienced by those at the two ends of the US's political spectrum.

Research has explored the effect of political ideology on consumption decisions, such as purchasing luxury products[3] and consumer-brand identification.[4] Political ideology is also a factor that may influence the degree to which people feel attached to a brand.[5]

Similar to political ideology, environmental ideology can also influence judgment. Consider, for instance, Greta Thunberg's environmental activist moves[6]. If you believe global warming is a real threat, you tend to support her. If you believe global warming isn't a concern, you're more likely to disagree with her. Either way, noise is involved in your judgment.

Besides the macro factors influencing our judgment, other factors, mostly micro ones, also contribute to the noise in judgment, such as experience, age, gender, and ethnicity. Another factor that can play a role in our judgment and attitude toward changing the status quo is our personality. By definition, a risk-averse person is going to be more worried about changing the status quo than an open-minded one.

Public Noise

While there is always noise in individual judgments, the level of noise is much higher in group judgments. Woke campaigns are judged publicly. Thus, individuals' judgments are often affected by social influence. The brand public can see how others are evaluating and judging a campaign, and that may affect their evaluation, overall adding to the degree of noise.

Recent studies and experiments have found that early reactions and responses to an online post can influence the popularity of the post. In some cases, we have seen a relatively homogenous response to woke campaigns, such as the widespread and bipartisan mockery directed toward Pepsi's and Starbucks' anti-racism campaigns[7].

Most people responded the same way, and the campaigns were quickly pulled. In those cases, the noise mostly came from the message, rather than the audience. However, in most cases of woke moves, the message divides the audience into for and against groups, polarizing the response.

Triggering the Noises

One mistake brands make is adopting a persona-identification approach and classifying the brand public into progressive versus conservative, woke versus un-woke, Democrat versus Republican. While such a classification benefits from simplicity, it adds to the noise, dilutes the message, and triggers the receiver's subconscious judgment noises. This is back to what I discussed under neutrality and inclusion. Brands shouldn't attack one group if they want to support another group. In other words, supporting misrepresented shouldn't mean attacking the overrepresented. Otherwise, there will be a great chance of resistance to status quo. To reduce the negative responses to their brand activism moves, brands should try to minimize the noise in receivers' judgment.

References

1   Kahneman, Daniel., Sibony, Olivier., and Sunstein, C. R. Noise. HarperCollins UK, 2022.

2   Bostock, B., 2018. *People are destroying their Nike shoes and socks to protest Nike's Colin Kaepernick ad campaign.* [online] *Business Insider.* September 4, 2018. https://www.businessinsider.com/nike-advert-wit h-colin-kaepernick-has-people-burning-products-2018-9

3   Kim, Jeehye Christine., Park, Brian., and Dubois, David. (2018). "How consumers' political ideology and status-maintenance goals interact to shape their desire for luxury goods." *Journal of Marketing*, *82*(6): 132–149.

4   Ordabayeva, Nailya., and Fernandes, Daniel. (2018). "Better or different? How political ideology shapes preferences for differentiation in the social hierarchy." *Journal of Consumer Research*, *45*(2): 227–250.

5   Chan, Eugene Y. and Ilicic, Jasmina. (2019). "Political ideology and brand attachment." *International Journal of Research in Marketing*, *36*: 630–646.

6   BBC. Two years of Greta—what impact has she had? *BBC Newsround, August 21, 2020.* https://www.bbc.co.uk/newsround/53816924.

7   Taylor, Kate. Howard Schultz reveals how he decided to launch Starbucks' 'embarrassing' and 'tone-deaf' 'Race Together' campaign despite internal concerns, *Business Insider.* Jan 29, 2019. https:// www.businessinsider.in/howard-schultz-reveals-how-he-decided-to-launch-starbucks-embarrassing-and-tone-deaf-race-together-camp aign-despite-internal-concerns/articleshow/67744688.cms

16

The Spotlight Moment
and Woke Spillover

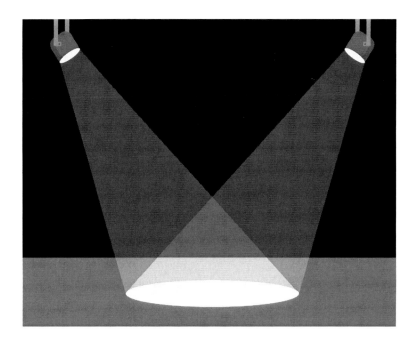

The Spotlight Effect

Among the nearly two hundred countries on this planet, if you close your eyes and think of a country associated with poor human rights practices, which one comes to mind? Now have a second guess and a third—and a fourth and a fifth. Did you think of Qatar, that small Middle Eastern nation? Would Qatar make it into your top twenty or even top fifty consideration? If you were a journalist, how likely do you think it would be for you to write about human rights abuses in Qatar given all the countries you could write about?

Few non-Qataris give much thought to Qatar or its human rights record in the normal course of events. Yet when Qatar was announced as the host of FIFA 2022 World Cup, media outlets all over the world suddenly started writing articles about Qatar's poor treatment of guest workers and the LGBTQIA+ community. Do you think the most important event that Qatar has ever hosted or may ever host may come to catch them? Does being under the spotlight contribute to a country's human right practices?

Let's take another example. Can you think of a country with the world's so called "coolest dictator"? Again, have a few guesses. Was El Salvador one of your guesses? Probably not. But when El Salvador became the first country to make Bitcoin legal tender in September 2021, it was an unexpected move, described by *Time* magazine (and other international press) as an attempt to rebrand the country. In their analysis, *Time* dug deeper (now that there was public interest) and highlighted what was unfolding in El Salvador, placing the spotlight on the country's president, Nayib Bukele, and his authoritarian approach to governing, which undermined the structures of El Salvador's democracy.

This is what I call the spotlight moment. The advantage and disadvantage of making bold moves is that you get lots of attention. Consumers, journalists, and others then start digging deep to learn more about your business and your practices, history, mission, and vision.

As briefly mentioned in previous chapters, brands trying to benefit from the free PR by jumping on a woke bandwagon will make themselves more exposed to public attention and put the spotlight on themselves. Once the public is curious about a brand, they won't just pay attention to what the brand wants them to pay attention to. They will examine many of the brand's other practices and not just its recent woke move.

Getting woke may grab the attention of the target audience and increase online and dinner table conversations about a brand. However, those conversations may not be necessarily limited to the brand's recent woke move and may extend to its previously un-woke moves and practices.

So if a brand is not woke but pretends to be, it will be caught and grilled by the brand public. This can force the brand to stay true to its promises and start practicing wokeness, even though the brand was not initially planning to do so. That's where cancel culture, and callout culture, can come into play—to challenge the brand.

Spillover That Triggers Callout and Cancel Culture

Besides the spotlight moment, another factor that contributes to callout culture is the spillover of woke moves. If a brand concludes that to avoid the unintended consequences of being on the spotlight they should remain silent about social issues and focus on their typical products and offerings, then the bad news is that they could be hit with the spillover of woke move expectations from consumers.

The spillover effect is what happens when that part of the society and the brand public that is positively influenced and impressed by the woke moves of some brands call on other brands to follow suit and also support social causes.

Starting with those brands with similar positioning (mostly the initiator brand's key competitors), some members of the public will expect other market players to also use their power to advocate for change. The spillover effect is also the extension of the brand public's expectations of brands, with obvious and immediate need for revising and reviewing their practices, in particular the need for changing a logo or name, or character with racist connotations.

In the following chapter, I discuss a few examples of consumer callout that resulted in a rebrand.

References

1   Nugent, Ciara. El Salvador Is Betting on Bitcoin to Rebrand the Country—and Strengthen the President's Grip, *Time. October 1, 2021.* https://time.com/6103299/bitcoin-el-salvador-nayib-bukele/

17

Callout and Cancel Culture

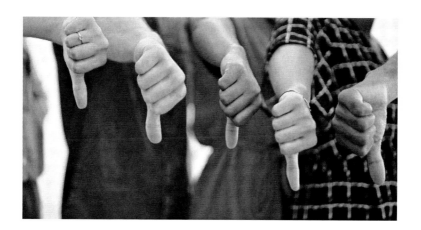

In the months following the first wave of the Black Lives Matter (BLM) movement, a new trend emerged. The public increasingly gravitated toward what came to be called callout and cancel culture. This was driven predominantly by the brand public—those eager to create, promote, and assign new values to a particular brand.

Thanks to the spillover effect of the BLM movement, the brand public is more aware than ever of social injustices, and no branding practices are immune from being called out.

While the world is getting used to the backlash toward woke marketing campaigns (for example, posting a black square on Instagram but engaging in no concrete measures in the fight against discrimination), cancel culture is moving into well-established branding practices, namely brand elements ranging from name and logo, to tagline, to brand characters.

However, the pressure from the brand public and the risk of cancelling a brand has been deemed too high to neglect. As a result, several brands under fire have rebranded, conforming to the public calls in an attempt to stay or become relevant to the brand public.

Such public cancel culture pressure may result in suboptimal decisions, in some cases rebranding or the retiring of iconic brands. The main question is whether the decisions announced by brands are the most effective in the fight against racism and discrimination and, going forward, what brands can learn from such moves.

Three iconic, fast-moving, consumer goods (FMCG) brands (Coon, Aunt Jemima, and Uncle Ben's) experienced public pressure and then chose to address issues around their branding.

Public Pressure on Brands

Coon

Launched in 1935, Coon was named after its founder, Edward William Coon. Over many decades, Coon cheese resisted the calls to change its name. Especially in the United States, coon, an abbreviation for racoon, is an offensive racial epithet for Black people. There was a failed attempt to have the brand name changed in 1999. In early 2021, in the wake of the BLM protests spreading to Australia, the name was finally changed to Cheer.

Retiring the market-leading brand within the hard cheese category (9 percent market share compared to Bega's 7.7 percent) can only be interpreted as a significant demonstration of anti-racism, one that would potentially reduce profits.

A little piece of cheese to some, and an iconic Australian food product to others, the Coon brand was built over decades and enjoyed significant consumer trust and loyalty.

Some brands, such as the music group Lady Antebellum (now Lady A), had more room and flexibility to partially revise their brand name in the wake of BLM. But Coon decided to exercise a wholesale brand overhaul.

The question remains whether the owners had other alternatives besides killing the name. Could the Coon brand have turned its challenge into an opportunity to combat racism?

Instead of dropping brand names altogether, would it be more beneficial to come up with new taglines and slogans that are more effective, as they can be used to adjust the negative connotation associated with the old name?[1] Could changing the stereotypical "coon" caricature have become Coon's higher purpose? Could Coon have dedicated a percentage of sales in anti-racist activism? Could buying Coon cheese have become a symbolic consumer behavior supporting the brand's (antiracist) purpose?

Aunt Jemima and Uncle Ben's

Since Aunt Jemima was launched in 1889, there have been several moves to revise the brand's perceived racist visual identity, such as replacing the handkerchief on the Aunt Jemima character's head with a plaid headband in 1968, to adding pearl earrings and a lace collar in 1989.

A costly move toward changing the brand character was deemed necessary once BLM emerged. Instead of retiring a category leader, PepsiCo (the owner of Aunt Jemima), had several opportunities to act as an agent of change. Aunt Jemima could have adopted the BLM movement when it was first created in 2013, its core purpose with a great fit, helping customers and employees to better understand the legacy of slavery, and supporting people of color.

The Uncle Ben's brand—a rice product launched in 1946 and named after an African American rice farmer—features "a beloved Chicago chef and waiter named Frank Brown" as part of its logo. According to the parent company, Mars,[2] rebranding Uncle Ben's as Ben's Original in 2020 was their way of responding to racial bias and injustices and standing in solidarity with the Black community.

In the case of Uncle Ben's and Aunt Jemima, some may see the brand rename as erasing history.

"I understand what Quaker Oats is doing because I'm Black and I don't want a negative image promoted. However, I just don't want her legacy lost, because if her legacy is swept under the rug and washed away, it's as if she never was a person," said relatives of former Aunt Jemima spokeswomen.[3]

More importantly, it can be seen as the conflict between advocating for diversity and fighting racism. On the one hand, brands are encouraged to celebrate diversity by hiring people of color and different ethnicities and to incorporate diversity in their marketing and branding communications. Yet there were calls to retire brands with Black visual identities. One argument that could be made is that leveraging the potential of an iconic brand like Aunt Jemima to fight racism could be more impactful than retiring the brand.

Chobani

A brand like Chobani, a leading yogurt brand founded by Hamdi Ulukaya, a Kurd from Turkey who immigrated to the United States, decided to go bold and adopt the story and history of its founder as the source of its brand purpose.

Chobani supports refugee entrepreneurs[4] through Chobani Incubator and actively hires refugees. Perhaps an Aunt Jemima or Uncle Ben's scholarship or foundation, financially supported by the brands' sales revenue, could have been introduced as a more proactive alternative response to fight against racism.

When brands don't play a proactive role, and act passively only in response to consumer callout, they are likely to make suboptimal decisions as they attempt to avoid controversy. Brands need to consider the spotlight and spillover effects of trying to be woke or deciding against it.

References

1   Hogan, Ruth. Cancel culture or offensive marketing? Brands from Coon to Coco Pops accused of racial insensitivity, *Inside FMCG*. June 17, 2020. https://insidefmcg.com.au/2020/06/17/cancel-cultur e-or-offensive-marketing-brands-from-coon-to-coco-pops-accused-of -racial-insensitivity/.

2   Uncle Ben's Brand Evolution. https://www.mars.com/news-and-stories/ press-releases/uncle-bens-brand-evolution

3   Aviles, Gwen. Relatives of Aunt Jemima actresses express concern history will be erased with rebranding, *NBC News,* June 20, 2020. https://www.nbcnews.com/pop-culture/pop-culture-news/relatives- aunt-jemima-actresses-express-concern-history-will-be-erased-n 1231769.

4   Lagorio-Chafkin, Christine., (2018) This Billion-Dollar Founder Says Hiring Refugees Isn't a Political Act, *Inc.* https://www.inc.com/magazine/201806/christine-lagorio/chobani-yogurt-hamdi-ulukay a-hiring-refugees.html.

18

The Woke Spectrum/Ladder

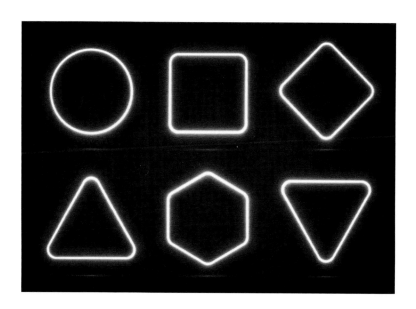

You may have heard the phrase "get woke, go broke," used mostly by those members of the brand public questioning the motivations of brands making woke moves.

However, the target of these accusations isn't just any woke brand. In fact, it's mostly those brands that do the minimum to signal they're woke. The skeptics argue that you (a brand) can't expect us (woke consumers) to fall in love with your surface-level costless signals. You can't expect us to believe that you're suddenly a social justice warrior just because you posted a black square on Instagram.

Part of the backlash against woke moves is a result of the lack of a clear and specific woke typology. As addressed earlier, posting a black square on Instagram won't make you a woke brand. Similarly, promising to be woke isn't equivalent to being woke. Also, you can't expect the brand public to praise a brand for a bunch of promises that may or may not happen in the distant future (for example, recruiting diverse talent over the next decade).

Therefore, this blanket term *woke*, which is used for any kind of activism progressive move, requires a more precise categorization. After studying different types of brand moves communicating a degree of wokeness, I explored a spectrum of four different types of woke brands:

- symbolizer and advocator;
- promiser;
- practicer; and
- sacrificer.

Most of the consumer backlash is directed at those woke brands doing the bare minimum and just making symbolic gestures. A brand needs to have a clear vison of how far it wants to go on the woke spectrum, and what type of woke it is planning to communicate and position around.

For many brands, as we saw over the past few years, it has been a bouncing-around practice, jumping on the woke bandwagon and then realizing they've exposed themselves to controversy and jumping off again. (Then, in most cases, quickly going back to their comfort zone). There is no shortage of brands that thought a simple Instagram post, or a tweet expressing solidarity with African Americans after the killing of George Floyd, would qualify them as a woke brand.

These brands might have saved themselves negative publicity if they had understood the woke brand spectrum.

Symbolizers/Advocators

At one end of the spectrum are the symbolizers. They always look for ways to symbolically signal they are alert to the injustices and discrimination found in society. Symbolizers find it easier to advocate for important issues than reflect on their own business practices. They want discrimination to stop and injustices to be fixed, but they rarely offer any solutions. Even when they do, it is not clear what their own contribution to solving the issue will be.

Symbolizers point the finger at everyone but themselves, vaguely blaming the system or lecturing the society about doing the right thing. They are good at making emotional statements and surfing the waves of the public's anger.

Symbolizers only come out of their shells when there is a social unrest and perhaps uprisings. The number of symbolizers is declining as the public is now more critical of symbolic, free-PR-generating moves, and will call symbolizer brands out.

Promisers

The second type of brand on the woke spectrum are those who have realized their brand image is being damaged because they are just making a symbolic attempt to address social issues. Their brand image will be further damaged, and they will be labelled opportunistic if they simply flipflop from the symbolic wokeness. Instead of reversing their symbolic woke move, promisers take a step further and move up the wokeness spectrum by starting to make woke promises.

For instance, when Adidas posted on their Instagram that they stand with the Black community after the killing of George Floyd, many accused the brand of not doing enough. Adidas, in a follow-up post, came back with a clear message to its audience: "We heard you." Adidas promised to make moves showing a commitment to tackling discrimination beyond a social media post. Adidas promised that thirty percent of any future recruitment in the United States would be from Black and Latino communities.

When YouTube announced they would donate $1 million to the Centre for Policing Equity, they experienced a backlash as $1 million was perceived as symbolic for a business with a $20 billion annual revenue. YouTube came back with a message telling its audience, "we heard you," and made several promises to take action.

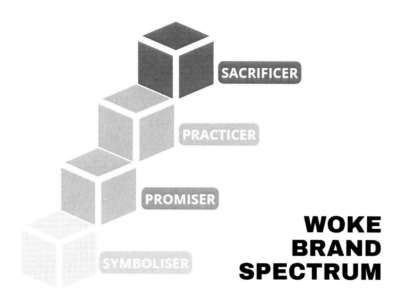

WOKE BRAND SPECTRUM

Practicer

A practicer often doesn't want to wait for the next social movement to arise to show how woke they are. Woke practicers have integrated the woke mindset in their ongoing practices and have a long-term approach to demonstrating they are woke and committed to fighting sociopolitical injustice.

A woke practicer can support a woke claim by showcasing their past woke moves. Practicers have a history of practicing diversity and inclusion in their talent recruitment, in their product range, marketing and branding campaigns and so forth. They're "talk walkers" who have built their woke image over time. Woke practicers not only advocate for equality, they have up-and-running equity policies in place, independent of recent sociopolitical movements, such as BLM or MeToo. Woke practicers are purpose-led brands that are not only purposeful in their communications, they're also purposeful in their internal practices. These types of brands are on the rise, as more and more brands are realizing the public's expectations won't be met without proof points of promise demonstration.

Sacrificers

This type of brand is prepared to go against conventional business wisdom and make moves that may risk their future revenue. Sacrificers are determined to assure the target audience they're committed and are prepared to stand for their values, even if it means making sacrifices.

The woke spectrum accommodates different types of wokeness, which can generate potentially different responses from the brand pubic. On paper, it is to be expected that when a brand migrates up the ladder from symbolizer to sacrificer, it attracts support and praise from the brand public. The more the brand public perceives the move costly and impactful, the greater the support should be.

However, given the divisive nature of many sociopolitical issues, and public's cynical views toward brands engaging in such issues, even a costly move may not necessarily be received well by the audience.

19

Woke Vision Triangle

To avoid making random decisions, brands need to have a clear vision about their woke moves going forward.

While it is convenient to sit back, go with the flow, and act as a conformer, it is also the riskiest approach: one that can lead to backlash. A one-off approach to becoming socially responsible and woke, and then bouncing back to being non-woke, not only damages the brand's reputation, it damages the woke concept in general.

If a brand is genuine, and sees itself as a woke brand going forward, it will need to have a clear, long-term vision that can guide future moves and practices. A well-informed, clear vision will prevent the brand from drifting aimlessly and having just a passive response to consumer call outs. A woke vision should tell a brand how far and deeply to get engaged in woke moves. A woke vision should also offer a synchronized connection between the brand's existing offering-focused vision and the woke vision.

Woke Vision Components

Type

Whether as a brand you're picturing yourself as an entity that is going to be a symbolizer and advocator, promiser, practicer, or even sacrificer, as part of your vison development, you'll need to choose the type of woke you're prepared to commit to.

In chapter 18 we looked at different types of wokeness. Perhaps the most important question for brands is choosing their woke type. Brands need to determine whether they will consider going from symbolic moves to substantially practicing, or going from a practicer to a sacrificer, and which involves the greatest degree of financial risk.

Focus

Once a brand has decided on its woke type, the next question is what the approach should be to demonstrate their wokeness. Is it going to focus on one issue, one region, or one target audience? Or will it be open to any issue, any region, and any target audience? At this point, a brand may choose to adopt a spotlight approach, a floodlight approach, or a hybrid approach.

Spotlight versus Floodlight

A brand's vision should indicate whether it is planning to have a general focus on issues, what I call a floodlight approach, or if it will focus on a specific cause and dedicate all its resources to address this issue over time, which I call a spotlight approach. Often those choosing the spotlight approach over floodlight can find a connection between a specific cause, the organization's history and story, the relevance of the offering, and the main target audience profile and persona.

Brands can also take a hybrid approach and combine both spotlight and floodlight. In this case, a brand may first put the spotlight on a certain group within a community (for example, young African Americans), then adopt a floodlight approach, addressing the range of issues that community is experiencing (such as police brutality and discriminatory hiring practices).

For instance, Gillette, which mainly makes products for men, could first adopt the spotlight approach and focus on issues related to its main target audience. It could then take a floodlight approach and focus on issues such as men's mental health, nontoxic masculinity, and stereotypical portrayals of men (floodlight).

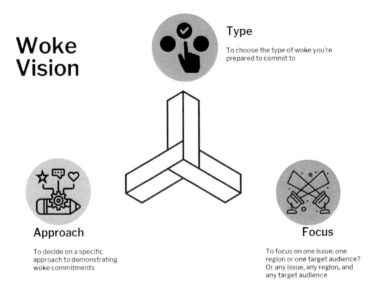

Woke Vision

Type
To choose the type of woke you're prepared to commit to

Approach
To decide on a specific approach to demonstrating woke commitments

Focus
To focus on one issue, one region or one target audience? Or any issue, any region, and any target audience

No matter what ambitions a brand may have for being woke, be it changing the world, breaking social barriers, fighting stigma, or celebrating diversity and inclusion, it will need to decide on a specific approach to demonstrating its woke commitment.

Woke Advocates: Inspire Society

This vison is mostly adopted by brands when their values and concerns are mostly unrelated to their offerings. Regardless of whether they sell ice-cream or are a car manufacturer, these brands initiate programs around peacemaking, social justice, marriage equality, and so forth.

For instance, you can be a soft drink brand and care about harassment against women. That's what Schweppes did (in their "Dress to Respect" campaign). A soft drink brand decided to go beyond the core focus of its offering and advocate for an issue that was not obviously related to that offering. With this approach, a brand can engage in any conversation and contribute to any debate.

Changing the World via Offerings

This group's vison is to change the world by making impactful products and offering services that influence the society. While every offering should be appealing and have an effect in general (otherwise it would disappear and be discounted over time), making products and offering services that directly contribute to social justice and equality is a major promise that brands adopting this approach should demonstrate.

Black is an app supported by Apple's Entrepreneur Camp for Black Founders and Developers program (a program led by underrepresented developers). The Black app aims to inspire the Black and Brown communities by collecting news about the world's greatest influencers of black culture.

If demonstrated and achieved, this approach can be the most effective way a business can contribute to wokeness. A great link and alignment between the offering and wokeness, with high relevance to what the brand public expects from a commercial brand can be an effective recipe for changing the world via offerings and services. The entertainment industry for instance has significantly shifted its focus toward creating content that aims to increase awareness about social issues, better representing the society, and giving voice to those who are underrepresented, and supporting progressive values.

Nike's FlyEase shoe is another example of making a change through products and services. FlyEase is the first hands-free shoe "with technology developed from insights from the disability community."

Going beyond communication and involving other components of marketing principles and branding elements, can significantly improve the brand public's perceptions toward a brand's woke motivations.

Victoria's Secret's recent inclusive cast of angels is an example of going beyond talk and starting to walk the talk. While Victoria's Secret's motivations can still be questioned and labelled as "embarking on diversity initiatives," it is still a small step in the right direction, benefiting future generations.

20

Woke Strategy Implementation

I have often been asked by media and industry practitioners about the dos and don'ts of woke execution. As discussed in previous chapters, several factors may have contributed to consumer perceptions toward brands' engagement in woke activism. Factors such as authenticity, practice, motivation, the degree of alignment, and sacrifice.

However, less is known about the way brands execute their message, and the strategies they use in communicating their messages. This is evident from reviewing publicly available user generated comments. For instance, while the brand public agrees with the brand on the importance of the issue the campaign tries to address, they still have reservations about the way brands execute their messages.

While some of the components of a conventional marketing campaign may apply to woke brand activism campaigns, there are other factors that need to be considered when planning and executing a woke campaign. This is because of the differences that exist between woke controversial messaging and non-woke, noncontroversial communications.

In this final chapter, I offer a checklist of woke elements to be considered for planning and implementing woke messages.

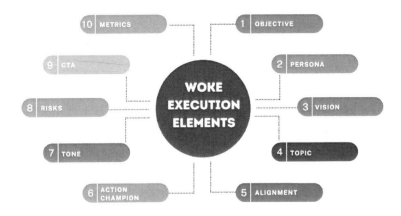

Woke Elements for Planning and Implementation

Woke elements	Considerations
Persona	• Who are the primary target audience you're trying to impress? • Who is the message directed at? Are you targeting functionality seekers, personality alignment driven, or purposeful or woke consumers? • What are the sociopolitical ideologies of the target audience?
Vision: Approach	• What is your approach to wokeness? • Are you going to focus on advocate and inspire messaging, highlighting the sociopolitical issues in your campaigns and woke moves? • Are you considering going beyond advocate and communicate to involve other marketing components and branding elements in your wokeness? • Are you going to redesign your products toward a more inclusive representation of society? • Are you going to develop products and services targeted toward those affected by discrimination, and those who are underrepresented?
Vision: Focus	• Is your focus going to be spotlight, floodlight, or hybrid? • Are you going to focus on a single issue or a variety of issues? • How connected are those issues going to be?
Vision: Type	• Are you going to be a • symbolizer; • promiser; • practicer; or • sacrificer?

Topic	• What topics and issues will you address (such as legal, environmental, social, or political)? • Do those topics have relevance to your target audience? • What is the rationale for the choice of topic? • Is your choice of topic going to be based on the degree of impact on your target audience? • Is your choice of topic going to be based on the topic's degree of social currency?
Personality alignment	• What are your preexisting brand personalities and images, and what is the link between your perceived personality and your new woke image? • Will it be an easy transfer of knowledge, or an extension of a previously formed image and brand knowledge to the new woke image?
Action champion	• Who is the champion and the hero of your woke move? • Is the hero internal or external? • Are you championing your products, services, or human capital as part of the solution to address the issue?
Objective	• What are your main objectives of getting woke? • Is your objective financial or nonfinancial? • If financial, are you setting short-term versus long-term objectives? • Is this a new growth strategy appealing to new target audiences, or reenergizing to better connect with your existing audience? • Are you focusing on awareness about the issue? • Are you informing the audience about the steps you're taking to address the issue?

Metric	• How are you going to measure success?
	• Are you going to rely on traditional metrics to examine the outcomes of your woke moves?
	   o Subjective versus behavioral?
	   o Financial versus nonfinancial?
	• What degree of backlash will there be?
	• Should the metric be related to your brand (i.e., the effect of the woke move on your brand performance)? Or should it be focused on the issue (i.e., the extent to which the woke move generated awareness for the social issue)?

Calls to action (CTA)	• Are you calling out the public and lecturing them? • What do you expect the audience to do in response to your message? • What is your call to action? • How do you want them to engage and participate in your woke initiative?
Risks	• Floodlight approach: What is the risk of confusing the target audience when switching from one issue to another? • Topic: What is the risk of choosing a topic unrelated to your core business focus? Would that come across as a strategy to deviate the discussion from your pain points to safer issues, with no relevance to your business? • Alignment: What is the risk of misalignment between your existing brand personality and image, and the new woke initiative? What is the risk of diluting consumer perceptions toward your brand?
Tone	• Are you dramatizing the issue? • Are you exaggerating? • Is the tone and the language overpowering? • Are you triggering resistance and therefore shutting off the target audience's engagement? • Are you attacking the target audience? • Are you lecturing the audience?

APPENDIX A

COVID-19 Pandemic and Purposefulness

Like hurricane Katrina turning Walmart into a purposeful organization, COVID-19 has turned brands into community brands practicing higher purpose values. Since early 2020, many brands have been making decisions to show that they can go beyond profit, and care for the community's wellbeing. This has turned them into brands that rise to the task and support the societies in which they operate. Those practices, in most cases with no clear previous history of similar purposeful activities, has helped them build a positive brand image overnight, something that in normal circumstances would take much longer.

In the past, being a community brand with a concern for social responsibility was considered an optional choice for corporations. However, COVID-19 has encouraged brands to show social responsibility and commitment. Their efforts will not go unnoticed as it is now tough to dislike any of those brands that were actively engaged in responding to COVID-19 and which supported the community.

Some brands (such as Ford and LVMH, aka Moët Hennessy Louis Vuitton) switched to manufacturing health-related products, such as ventilators, face masks, and hand sanitizer. Some brands, such as Chipotle and Snapchat became super creative, coming up with events, programs, and ad campaigns that attempted to bolster mental health and keep the community motivated and resilient.

After studying more than one hundred brands' responses to COVID-19, I have classified the purposeful responses into four main categories:

- donations;
- adjusting marketing plans;
- producing healthcare equipment and devices; and
- employee-customer protection.

Donations

Donating toward the fight against COVID-19 was a common response to the pandemic. Unilever was among the first, announcing it would donate hygiene products to those in need. Other major brands, such as Kraft Heinz and Reckitt Benckiser made significant donations to charities.

Facebook announced it would donate $100 million to support small businesses with its Boost with Facebook program. Netflix announced it would donate $100 million to workers displaced as a result of COVID-19 halting work on movies and television series. Google announced it would donate $840 million-worth of free ad space to small- and medium-size business and partnered with Apple to create a COVID-19 tracking tool. McDonalds announced it would donate and distribute four hundred thousand masks. Coca-Cola donated the use of its social media platforms (Twitter, Facebook, and Instagram) to charities such as the American Red Cross and Salvation Army, to allow those charities use the brand's reach to support the community.

Adjusting Marketing Plans

That is, pulling existing ads and products and launching COVID-19-oriented ads and products. Several brands decided to make high-risk decisions, such as pulling their marketing campaigns to show social responsibility. These campaigns were often not in line with the social distancing and stay at home messages governments were broadcasting.

Silk paused its *Granbassador* campaign, which was based on searching for a brand ambassador and involved a two-week trip to Silk's headquarters. As this was deemed non-essential travel at the time, Silk decided to cancel the campaign. KFC was also forced to pull an ad that was heavily focusing on finger-licking messages. Cadbury pulled its Easter ad, as the brand recognized "it's no longer appropriate to encourage close physical contact."

Molson Coors cancelled the launch of an already planned campaign called "The official beer of working remotely" to avoid being perceived as insensitive and opportunistic.

Ford not only pulled a new vehicle ad, it replaced it with a campaign aimed at stopping the spread of COVID-19. To use another example, the beer brand Madison launched a new beer in response to COVID-19, called FVCK COVID.

Colgate announced they would start manufacturing a new soap, packaged with instructions on proper handwashing, echoing the World Health Organization's (WHO) #SafeHands message. Snapchat cancelled their scheduled events, exhibitions, and conferences and went on to indefinitely postpone its virtual summit. BMW cancelled its Ultimate Driving Experience event. The bearing of this type of brand response on fighting COVID-19 was mainly virtue signaling, showing the community that these brands were making ethical and responsible marketing decisions.

Donation

Donating towards the fight against COVID-19

Production

Producing healthcare equipment and devices

Marketing Plan

Pulling existing ads and products and launching COVID-19-oriented ads and products

Employee Protection

Employee-customer protection

Brands Response to Covid-19

Figure 1: Four categories of responses to COVID-19.

Producing Health-Care Equipment and Devices

Several brands responded by tackling the issue directly, offering support in forms of health-care products and services to those the most at risk.

This most frequently involved dedicating part of the production line to producing products such as soap, hand sanitizer, and face masks and donating these products to charities and health workers.

LVMH was one of the first corporations to announce it would dedicate part of it perfume and cosmetic production line to producing hand sanitizer. Anheuser-Busch InBev announced it would produce hand sanitizer in response to the growing need for it. Again, in response to the shortage of hand sanitizer, UK-based brewer, BrewDog, launched a new brand to produce a hand sanitizer called BrewGel.

P&G took similar action by announcing it would produce protective masks for health-care workers, and that these masks would be distributed around the world. Bosch developed a rapid COVID-19 test. Mattel stated it would produce face masks using material previously used to make clothes for Barbie dolls. Ford teamed up with GE and 3M to make lifesaving equipment, such as ventilators.

All these initiatives, which tackled the crisis directly and offered help to those on the frontline, were among the most impactful actions taken by brands to help save lives.

Employee-Customer Protection

During the difficult time of the COVID-19 crisis, many brands showed concern toward their customers, employees, and stakeholders.

Snapchat brought forward the launch of its new feature, "Here for you," which provides resources to those searching for mental-health-related topics. Chipotle offered "Chipotle Together" Zoom catch-ups, enabling fans to hang out and mingle with celebrities. Bud Light sponsored a virtual concert called "Home Edition," during which various pop stars performed live music. Brands such as Starbucks and Unilever extended benefits, deferred debts, and offered cash-flow relief to cushion the economic fallout of COVID-19 on customers, employees, suppliers, and stakeholders.

Typology of Brands Responding to COVID-19

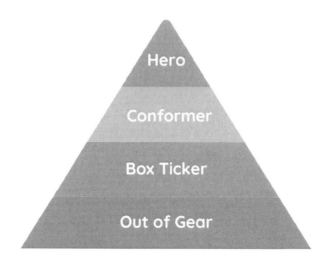

Based on their degree of impact and the continuous commitment to responding to the COVID-19 pandemic, I have classified brands into four main groups:

- heroes;
- conformers;
- box tickers; and
- out of gears.

Heroes

Brands that showed a great appetite for tackling the crisis and making decisions that have had a profound influence are heroes. Sincere, profit-sacrificing moves to tackle a crisis make a brand heroic.

Committed brands with impactful moves, and in particular with a low fit (based on the industry they are operating in), are the most likely candidates to become heroes. Hero brands have been able to go well beyond society's expectations, delivering on most or all of the elements of authenticity, by sacrificing profits and genuinely acting to address the crisis.

Conformers

Conformers are responsible brands that care for the community. However, unlike heroes, they were not prepared to take substantial steps, make impactful contributions, and provide continuous support to the wider society, or at least their stakeholders, throughout the crisis. This group of brands mostly aimed at meeting the expectations of the target audience and conforming to the social responsibility expected by the community, so as to avoid any potential backlash and call out.

Box Tickers

Box tickers responded to the crisis. However, the type of response they chose to support the community was often trivial and lacking in real power.

Brands offering "A letter from the CEO" or "We're here to help" messages to customers, without offering crisis-specific support packages, fall into this category of box-ticking brands.

Box tickers are passive conformers, doing the bare minimum to remain in the list of brands responding to the crisis. There are several reasons for choosing to do the bare minimum. While the lack of financial resources may justify small- and medium-sized brands choosing to be box tickers, for major global brands, box-ticker moves suggest a lack of belief and determination in demonstrating social responsibility and purposefulness.

Out of Gears

High-profile brands with large presence in our normal lives were put to the test during the pandemic. Would they come to rescue the community? Offer some sort of support to cushion the blow and stand by their consumers?

Out of gear brands are those established, financially successful brands that failed to respond and use their capabilities (financial, technological, and logistic, for example) to fight the pandemic. Out of gear brands with clear image and positioning in consumers' minds are at the highest risk of being called out and receiving backlash from their target audience if they do not live up to expectations, or even worse, if their actions are perceived as exploitative.

Adidas, for instance, generated a backlash because its legal (but tin-eared) decision to take advantage of relief packages offered by government and skip the rental payments on its retail stores. In terms of ethics, this was seen as cynically exploiting the crisis given a strong brand like Adidas, with its $2 billion in annual net profit, was expected to help fight the crisis by making impactful moves to support the community, rather than using to COVID-19 to lower its expenses.

APPENDIX B

The Woke Ad That Shook the Marketing World

On August 14, 2016, during a preseason match, Colin Kaepernick (at the time a football quarterback, now a civil rights activist) chose not to stand during the national anthem to protest police brutality and social injustice. Kaepernick did not know he was going to change the world of marketing and advertising, forcing it to move toward more purposeful and woke messages and content. It was a turning point for advertisers to flip around the obsession with the typical outputs (number of clicks, ad skip rate, and sales generation, among other factors) and be more focused on the input, the messages they should communicate, and the influence they should have on society.

Maybe the world doesn't need another ad about the fifth camera at the back of your smartphone. Maybe offering multiple versions of just one car model (BMW 3 series) only adds to the choice fatigue and post-purchase anxiety. Maybe the response to Nespresso's famous "What Else?" campaign series (featuring George Clooney) isn't "nothing," and maybe instead of focusing on the quality of coffee in their campaigns, Nespresso should focus on the quality of the lives of the coffee farmers they are accused of neglecting. Maybe you can be a chocolate brand and launch ad campaigns that are not focused on happy life moments and celebrations but instead about domestic violence, a topic that on the surface seems irrelevant to a cholate brand.

It was a turning point for brands to start getting comfortable with questioning the status quo in consumers' ideologies and marketing practices.

Nike, a brand with a history of pushing for sociopolitical change and fighting discrimination and stigma, realized this was the moment for their next big move. Nike's campaigns have addressed ageism (1988); supported people with disabilities (1989); supported the LGBTQI+ community by featuring an HIV-positive gay athlete (1995); and tackled gender issues with If You Just Let Me Play (1995), Voices (2012), and Equality (2017), which featured Black athletes Lebron James and Serena Williams. Nike's most talked about campaign came in 2018 with Dream Crazy and Dream Crazier, demonstrating that the brand has been inclusive in addressing social issues over time and fighting against prejudice.

Nike's Dream Crazy campaign including a two-minute film featuring the stories of sixteen athletes with inspirational woke stories and narrated by Colin Kaepernick. The theme of the campaign was, "Don't ask if your dreams are crazy. Ask if they're crazy enough," and the content showed how the power of sports can move the world forward. The campaign shocked and shook the corporate world—perhaps it was the first time a brand went against conventional business wisdom and partners with a controversial figure. Like the previous heroes of the Nike's progressive campaigns, Colin Kaepernick has a story to tell; however, he is a polarizing figure, given that his method of protesting social injustice (first sitting and then kneeling during the national anthem) was politically charged.

Fast-forward to 2021, three years after the launch of Nike's Dream Crazy, the campaign that won the inaugural World's Most Effective Commercial award at the Effie Awards. While we can follow the tradition of the past hundred years of advertising, getting technical about the elements of success for this ad, the lesson here for the next generation of advertisers and creative directors is simple. Instead of discussing the episodic storytelling, or nonclassical narrative, or stencil directing, or stylistic congruity, focus on people not products and place your message in the context of purposeful human value-oriented messages.

"We have seen Nike following its sportsmanship and showing humanistic care and beliefs for diverse communities, even when encountering resistance and difficulties. It is, indeed, a beautiful, powerful, and most importantly, an effective case that is worthy of the Iridium Effie"—Helen Luan (Tencent), Global Best of the Best Effie Co-Chair.

However, such campaigns aren't easy to execute and not recommended for all brands to adopt. Only a handful of brands may feel confident in using such high-tension messages and figures in their campaigns. Brands that don't have any history of wokeness, or pushing social justice and fighting discrimination, can end up with the least-effective campaigns, which may be pulled and followed by apologies.

Many brands have become overexcited about their social responsibility overnight, and drifted from selling shampoos to selling virtue, from selling sugary water to becoming a peacemaker (Pepsi's campaign featuring Kendal Jenner was accused of trivializing the BLM movement)[1], from selling coffee to discussing race inequality (such as Starbucks' Race Together campaign)— both campaigns were pulled and apologies were issued. While getting the messages right and turning an idea into a successful campaign are important, priority should be given to not getting it wrong.

Nike's campaign was effective not because it generated greater revenue or higher product-related engagement. It was effective because it had an effect on the conversation about important issues of society and humanity. The most important (but hidden) lesson to be learned from Nike's Dream Crazy campaign is its success wasn't the outcome of a two-minute carefully written, inspiring, and thought-provocative narrative. It was the outcome of collective, consistent, and continuous messaging aligned with the image the brand has created and positioned over years.

References

1   Victor, Daniel. Pepsi Pulls Ad Accused of Trivializing Black Lives Matter, *The New York Times*, April 5, 2017.
    https://www.nytimes.com/2017/04/05/business/kendall-jenner-pepsi-ad.html

AUTHOR BIOGRAPHY

Abas Mirzaei holds a PhD in marketing and is an assistant professor (Senior Lecturer) at Macquarie Business School. His area of expertise is branding, woke marketing, and brand activism. His work has been published in academic journals. His work on 'woke' branding has appeared in several media outlets such as The Conversation, Inside Retail, Inside FMCG, SBS, NITV, ABC News, BBC Radio, SMH, Marketing Magazine, Mumbrella, AdNews, Medium, and many others. Abas is the winner of the Emerald Literati Award: Outstanding Paper, *European Journal of Marketing,* 2022.